THIS BOOK BELONGS TO:

_____

PILGRIM

RUTH CHOU SIMONS

HARVEST HOUSE PUBLISHERS
EUGENE, OREGON

Published in association with William K. Jensen Literary Agency, 119 Bampton Court, Eugene,
OR 97404

Original artwork by Ruth Chou Simons; design work by Sarah Alexander Schools

Cover and interior design by Janelle Coury

For bulk, special sales, or ministry purchases, please call 1-800-547-8979.
Email: Customerservice@hhpbooks.com

 This logo is a federally registered trademark of the Hawkins Children's LLC. Harvest House Publishers, Inc., is the exclusive licensee of
this trademark.

PILGRIM

Copyright © 2023 by Ruth Chou Simons (art and text)
Published by Harvest House Publishers
Eugene, Oregon 97408
www.harvesthousepublishers.com

ISBN 978-0-7369-8292-4 (hardcover)

Library of Congress Control Number: 2022945987

Printed in China

23 24 25 26 27 28 29 30 31 / RDS / 10 9 8 7 6 5 4 3 2 1

TO MY FELLOW PILGRIMS:

HIS GRACE HAS BROUGHT US
SAFE THUS FAR,
AND HIS GRACE WILL
LEAD US HOME.

CONTENTS

A LONG ENDURANCE

NEARING HOME

OUR PILGRIM JOURNEY

I don't know about you, but sometimes I find myself in such a hurry or so focused on where I'm going that I miss the street signs meant to point the way and help me discern where I am. I get lost, miss the turn, or think I'm somewhere I'm not—all because I'm not paying attention to the very guideposts meant to inform my journey.

A guidepost, by definition, points the way on a path that may be difficult or hard to navigate. Sometimes the way of the Christian life seems unclear or complex. Sometimes our walk with Christ feels like an unsure road to understand. But the Bible, God's Word, is a lamp to our feet and a light for our path, as we read in Psalm 119:105. We've not been left to wander aimlessly on this journey heavenward. No, our Savior shows us the way, by being the Way, the Truth, and the Life (John 14:6).

I wrote this *Pilgrim* journey so that we might walk this road, courageously and confidently, together as Christ-followers. Through the guideposts of grace that appear in this book—guideposts that affirm key truths in the Bible—we will find that we are not alone, not abandoned, and no longer need to strive to secure our own footing or define our own paths. Instead, we discover that God writes our stories, paves our paths, leads the way, never leaves us nor forsakes us, and goes with us wherever this earthly journey takes us.

Here, we'll explore reminders from Scripture that point us forward on our journey with Christ—guideposts that direct our hearts and minds to the truths of the gospel, the attributes of God, and the core foundations of our faith. We'll encounter reminders of God's character and how He leads us onward as pilgrims—the same reminders that have shaped believers who've gone before us in ages past. Some of these faithful pilgrims penned hymns that elucidate these truths in ways that stick with us long after the melodies fade; these accompany us on this journey as well.

My prayer is that through this exploration, you'll discover the themes of grace that punctuate not only the moment of salvation in a believer's life, but all the twists and turns, hills and valleys that shape our journeys—before, behind, ahead, and along the way. These truths are reminders of *God's* way, not yours or mine. They are indicators of God's story, not our own. Lord willing, these guideposts of grace will serve to remind us, again and again, season after season, that God is at work right where we are.

If you're weary, fellow traveler, I'm here to tell you you're not alone, and there is great hope for the road ahead. I'm here to remind you that you can lay down the heavy burden you've been carrying for miles and miles, and—if you're willing—let your Savior carry it for you instead. He is at work more than you know. There are guideposts of grace everywhere we look, friend, and they accompany our *Pilgrim* journey, even now. We just have to cultivate eyes that see and hearts that believe these guideposts are ours—for me and for you. Will you join me—as God leads us onward in this *Pilgrim* journey, together?

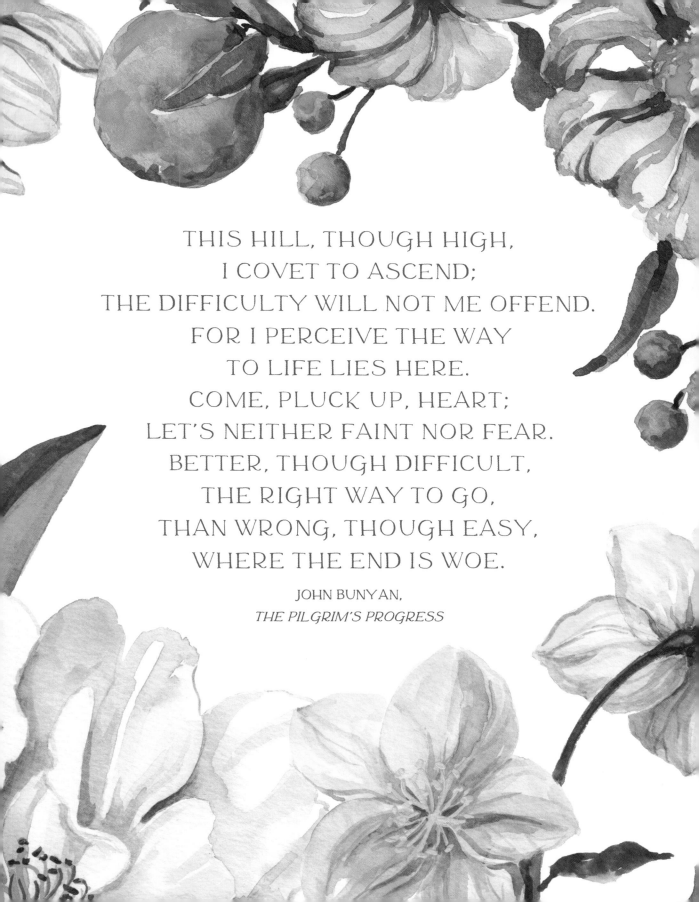

THIS HILL, THOUGH HIGH,
I COVET TO ASCEND;
THE DIFFICULTY WILL NOT ME OFFEND.
FOR I PERCEIVE THE WAY
TO LIFE LIES HERE.
COME, PLUCK UP, HEART;
LET'S NEITHER FAINT NOR FEAR.
BETTER, THOUGH DIFFICULT,
THE RIGHT WAY TO GO,
THAN WRONG, THOUGH EASY,
WHERE THE END IS WOE.

JOHN BUNYAN,
THE PILGRIM'S PROGRESS

THE JOURNEY BEGINS

*My name is now Christian,
but my name used to be Graceless.*

John Bunyan, *The Pilgrim's Progress*

O love
of God,
how rich
and pure!
How measureless
and strong!

1

A LOVE THAT WILL
NEVER LEAVE YOU

My firstborn spent a semester abroad in his junior year of college. Like any mom who's separated from her child, I knew the exact distance between him and me those months he was away. It felt like a million miles, but it was actually only 4,533, including one very large body of water. While he was away, we weren't even on the same continent, and truthfully, I hadn't expected the ache to be so overwhelming. Thankfully, our weekly chats on video eased the sadness and served to remind me that, in spite of miles and time zones, there was no distance between our hearts.

Every journey is marked by distance and terrain. Distance tells you how far you have yet to go, and terrain indicates how much effort it'll take to get to your destination. When traveling, we know we will be separated from comforts and the people we know and love, and we plan accordingly. In preparation for a journey, we pack survival kits, emergency contact cards, and try to minimize the unsettledness we inevitably experience when we're far from home.

It's not so different with our spiritual journeys. Whether we feel distant from or in close proximity to the things that give us assurance can be the difference between journeying in fear and anxious striving, or journeying from a position of courage and confidence.

We were made for the latter in our walks with God—a journey that traverses seasons of life and the difficult terrain of our hearts. It's a journey that finds its purpose when we receive the gift of salvation through Christ and live as a new creation the rest of our days until we see our Savior face to face. The promises recorded for us in the Bible testify that while the journey is not easy, we do not walk alone.

So why do so many of us feel distant and alone? Why do we so often allow ourselves to believe that the distance between the God who rescues us and our sinful hearts is vast, when Christ erased the miles, the distance, and the eternal separation sin causes...and brought us near?

Maybe that's why the apostle Paul so clearly addresses the true state of a Christ-follower's nearness to God, and wrote in Romans 8:38-39, "I am sure that neither death nor life, nor angels nor rulers, nor things present nor things to come, nor powers, nor height nor depth, nor anything else in all creation, will be able to separate us from the love of God in Christ Jesus our Lord."

Paul wouldn't have spelled out all the ways we cannot be separated from God's love if it wasn't so easy to forget. As if death, angels, and rulers were not enough, Paul says "nor anything else in all creation" (read: nothing in all the world) is capable of removing us from the active love of God in our lives as believers.

Let that sink in for just a moment...

You are loved.
  You are welcomed.
   Nothing can get in the way of God's love for you.
    Not even you.
     Not the government.
     Not evil.
     Not even your own mistakes.
     God's love is so limitless that no one can stop it.

My guess is that, like me, it's much easier for you to remember the ways you've caused distance with God than to remember the ways God has bridged the impossible chasm with His love. That's why Paul makes such a dramatic point about the inability for anything to remove you from God's love.

THE LOVE OF GOD IS GREATER FAR
THAN TONGUE OR PEN CAN EVER TELL;
IT GOES BEYOND THE HIGHEST STAR,
AND REACHES TO THE LOWEST HELL.
THE WAND'RING CHILD IS RECONCILED
BY GOD'S BELOVED SON.
THE ACHING SOUL AGAIN MADE WHOLE,
AND PRICELESS PARDON WON.

For I am sure that neither death nor life, nor angels nor rulers, nor things present nor things to come, nor powers, nor height nor depth, nor anything else in all creation, will be able to separate us from the love of God in Christ Jesus our Lord.

ROMANS 8:38-39

THE LOVE OF GOD

God's love is a core aspect of His character—so much so that the Bible says God is love. His love is perfect, steadfast, and not based on feelings or emotions. God exhibits His love in ways that are in harmony with His holiness, justice, omnipotence, and other attributes. One special quality of God's love is that it's self-sacrificing. He was willing to send His Son to die on the cross for us so that we could be brought back into relationship with Him.

In his letter to the Romans, Paul teaches that God secured our salvation by grace, and not because of our righteousness or religious acts. He shows that it was God's love that fulfilled the law we are unable to keep. It was God's love that rescued us, and it is God's love that sustains us. As Christ-followers, we can't walk, follow, or go anywhere with Jesus if we don't first surrender to the love of God that makes our journey with Him possible in the first place.

How might you think differently about your relationship with God this day if you took to heart the words of this hymn writer?

> *The love of God is greater far*
> *than tongue or pen can ever tell;*
> *it goes beyond the highest star,*
> *and reaches to the lowest hell.*
> *The wand'ring child is reconciled*
> *by God's beloved Son.*
> *The aching soul again made whole,*
> *and priceless pardon won.*

Does God still seem distant when you consider the distance He traversed to rescue you?

Without wonder and amazement for God's love for us, we will continue to live as if we're separated from our Father by millions of miles. Without recognizing the nature of God's love, we'll believe we've stayed away from church too long to darken the doors and take part in Sunday worship. We'll assume we're too far off His radar to even know His care. We'll act as though we walk alone, far from home. Don't believe these lies, friend. Instead, be amazed by the limitless love of God. As Samuel Rutherford so wisely said, "Believe God's love and power more than you believe your own feelings and experiences. Your rock is Christ, and it is not the rock that ebbs and flows but the sea."

Nothing can separate us from God's love because His love doesn't depend on us or our feelings. It's limitless and unending, and is in perfect harmony with His goodness, mercy, and justice. It's not fickle. He's not holding out on us. We don't have to worry for the other shoe to drop. Because God's love for us is infinite, our security in Him is infinite. Let that truth usher total assurance and peace into your worry-torn heart. You and I get to choose right now to realign our hearts with the truth of His love for us. It's deeper, wider, more extravagant than we know. God's love has eradicated the distance between our hearts and His; we have a forever companion who will stay at our side through every step of life's journey.

When we could not be home with God, Christ became *God with us* on this journey. God with us...*home* with us. The very gift of salvation is that we might walk with God, forever.

GUIDEPOST:

NOTHING CAN SEPARATE US FROM GOD'S LOVE.

NEVER *did* HIS *love* BEGIN AND NEVER CAN IT CEASE. *It is from eternity and shall be to eternity.*

C. H. SPURGEON

Amazing grace!
how sweet the sound
that saved a wretch
like me! I once was
lost but now am
found, was blind,
but now I see.

2

GRACE FOR EVERY STEP OF THE JOURNEY

Imagine yourself on a steep and narrow mountain trail, with precarious cliffs and drop-offs along the path. The trail is rocky and difficult to navigate. At times, loose rock and dirt crumble along the edge and roll downward, and you suddenly realize just how far the chasm is below. Gusts of wind come along and you reach for something secure—a branch, a tree trunk, more solid ground. You ask yourself, *Will I make it?*

But what if there was a sturdy rope securely fastened along every point of this trail from beginning to end? What if the course was mapped out at the start, and regardless of difficulty, the secure and steady rope guided the course all the way to your destination? This tether of rescue is the grace of God.

I don't know about you, but sometimes I forget why God's grace is all that amazing. I forget that it's the lifeline that holds me fast to my eternal welcome with my heavenly Father. How quickly I forget...

> when I hide my sin and attempt to clean up my life before drawing near to the Lord.
> when I try to prove I'm worthy of God's love by doing and serving more.
> when I'm fearful and try to control my life circumstances for my own good.
> when I don't rest, believing my trying a little harder will somehow fix my life.

THE GRACE OF GOD

God's grace is the expression of His goodness toward those who deserve punishment. He freely extends His favor to people by offering them salvation from their sins. This grace is generously bestowed on the undeserving and cannot be earned. God's grace is also endless—the gift of salvation is eternal and cannot be lost, which means our future arrival in heaven is guaranteed.

These attempts to save myself are but a frantic weaving of a rope with straw and weeds when God offers a lifeline so strong and securely tethered to Himself that we need nothing but to walk with Him.

The apostle Paul never minced words; he always told it like it was, and I so appreciate that about him. You know he chose his words carefully, and because all Scripture is inspired by God, we can also trust that those words were carefully chosen by Him. So when Paul said in Ephesians 2:8-9, "By grace you have been saved through faith. And this is not your own doing; it is the gift of God, not a result of works, so that no one may boast," he was making this point to the believers reading his letter: God did not rescue you on account of your good deeds.

Do you know what that means, friend? It means that you can never be holy enough, strong enough, religious enough, or self-disciplined enough to not need the grace of God. We can stop trying to clean up or fix up our lives first before surrendering to Jesus.

The stream
of grace
and
righteousness

IS DEEPER AND BROADER
THAN THE STREAM OF
GUILT.

MATTHEW HENRY

Perhaps the idea of trying harder and the false promises that lead to striving have left you weary and exhausted. Trying harder through personal achievement and religious effort was the continual ball and chain of the ancient world before the cross of Christ. In many ways, it still is today. What was so amazing about the coming of Christ? Why would the Messiah mean freedom to an enslaved people? The Jews expected a Deliverer who would right every wrong and free them from political tyranny. But God's plan was to offer so much more. God's plan was to send a Deliverer who would right every wrong for eternity and free all who believe so they no longer remain under the tyranny of sin and death.

Christ did not come to worthy, loyal, faith-focused people; they were not deserving. In fact, Jesus came in the midst of self-righteous religiosity. He came to a world that, for the most part, didn't even want what He was offering. But God sent Christ to reconcile us to Himself when we lacked the ability to truly reconcile with one another. God sent Jesus—the only one who was undeserving of God's justice toward sin—to bear what we couldn't: "For our sake he made him to be sin who knew no sin, so that in him we might become the righteousness of God" (2 Corinthians 5:21). Christ bore the punishment we deserved so that He could accomplish what we couldn't: righteousness and favor with God. That's what makes God's grace so amazing, and we will miss it if we still think we can save ourselves.

Listen, friend. That feeling that you're not enough? That sense that you may not have what it takes? It's a good place to start if it leads you to discover all that God desires to produce in you through grace. Lack and inability describe our condition apart from Christ. Abundance and equipped are the marks of a life tethered to the grace of God.

> *Amazing grace! how sweet the sound*
> *That saved a wretch like me!*
> *I once was lost but now am found,*
> *Was blind, but now I see.*

When these words become more than familiar Sunday morning lyrics, and instead become our declaration of God's rescue in a lost life apart from Him, we finally begin to discover that we were never meant to journey alone; God's desire has been to walk with us ever since the Garden.

Because of God's grace, we have access to sure footing, access to nearness, access to full confidence that we do not walk this journey alone.

The tether of God's grace, which reaches into eternity past when God knew you before the foundation of the world, and extends all the way to eternity future, when you will dwell with God in heaven, runs all along that trail from start to finish. God's gift of grace—the eternal welcome secured for us through the life, death, and resurrection of Jesus Christ—replaces our attempts to hold on with a strong grip with God's ability to hold us with His steady hand. No wonder Carl Trueman said it this way: "It is because we are saved by grace that grace then works in our lives to accomplish God's purposes for us. The Christian life originates in God's grace and is lived by God's grace."[1] God's grace not only saves us *from* destruction, it saves us *for* redemptive purposes. Grace doesn't just transfer us from lost to found; it ensures that we never lose our way or eternal footing again.

Friend, there is not one moment of your life that is not held fast by the strong and mighty assurance of God's grace. No matter how bumpy, how treacherous, or how unknown, you will ascend from the valleys to the peaks not according to your own ability or strength, but because the rope of God's grace holds and guides you every step of the way to His presence.

GUIDEPOST:

GOD'S GRACE HOLDS AND GUIDES US EVERY STEP OF THE WAY TO HIS PRESENCE.

The Lord has
promised good to
me, His word
my hope secures;
He will my shield
and portion be
as long as life
endures.

What wondrous love is this, O my soul, O my soul! Christ laid aside His crown for my soul.

3

HIS MERCY ALWAYS DELIVERS YOU

Tree rings tell the story of a tree's life journey. Narrow, cluttered rings show signs of drought, while wide, evenly spaced rings tell a story of consistent sunlight and steady growth. When a forest fire scorches a tree, the flames leave a scar. The evidence of that event or season is recorded within the tree's layers; its rings forever tell of the time and severity of its brush with fire. And then other times, when harsh winds blow and a tree begins to lean, its core—the center of its rings—becomes off-centered. You see, tree rings tell of a tree's seasons of growth and seasons of turmoil.

You and I have layers upon layers to our stories as well. For most of us, there are pages here and there in our pilgrim story marked with regret, sadness, and shame. At times, what we hoped would be confined to one page ends up becoming several in the chapters of our lives. Those life events and circumstances have marked us. You and I don't have to have the same upbringing, family history, or life circumstances to agree this is true: that there are stages of our journey that we see better now in hindsight; and, if we're honest, wish we could rewrite.

You can likely call to mind some of the very choices that have affected the concentric rings of your life. When I think of certain seasons and circumstances, I remember how unlovely

31

and *unlovable* I felt when caught in the midst of the mess of my life. Sometimes it was a result of my own sin; sometimes it was on account of another's. When the scars and wounds of devastation leave their marks, healing and change may seem nearly impossible, especially when we feel unworthy of love.

But, when we read God's Word, we see a different point of view when it comes to desperation and being at the end of ourselves; we learn of a mercy we don't always understand. The prophet Micah wrote, "Who is a God like you, who pardons sin and forgives the transgression of the remnant of his inheritance? You do not stay angry forever but delight to show mercy" (Micah 7:18 NIV). It may not seem like a gift of grace to be brought low and to feel unworthy in our desperation and need, but it is in that very condition we are made aware of God's merciful love for us.

Would you consider God's love wondrous and merciful if you had never known how unsatisfying and void your pursuits are without Him?

Could we grasp how merciful God is if we didn't experience how undeserving we are in our rebellion and foolishness?

The apostle Paul, the "chief of sinners" as he called himself, met the Lord at the ugliest point of his rebellion and self-righteousness. God literally stopped Paul on his path of destruction and humbled him both physically and spiritually. In His holiness, God could have crushed Paul (also known as Saul) in his sin, but He didn't. Instead, God's mercy rescued Paul while he was in his most unlovely state and made Paul His own—giving him a new identity. Paul was no longer a persecutor, Pharisee, legalist, and self-righteous; he was now a servant, missionary, changed, and one who boasted in his weakness. And it was this same Paul who defined the very essence of God's mercy for those rescued by the cross of Christ:

> God shows his love for us in that while we were still sinners, Christ died for us (Romans 5:8).

Notice these words: *While...still sinners...*

Paul was making a point. In fact, he was making the same point he made in Ephesians 2:1-6:

GOD SHOWS HIS LOVE
FOR US IN THAT WHILE WE
WERE STILL SINNERS,
CHRIST DIED FOR US.

ROMANS 5:8

THE MERCY OF GOD

God's mercy speaks of His deep compassion and affection for those who are in misery or distress. Like His grace, God's mercy is freely given to those who are unworthy and undeserving. So great is His mercy that even when we were dead in our sins, He was willing to make us alive together with Christ. And His mercies never end; they are new every morning.

> You were dead in the trespasses and sins in which you once walked, following the course of this world, following the prince of the power of the air, the spirit that is now at work in the sons of disobedience—among whom we all once lived in the passions of our flesh, carrying out the desires of the body and the mind, and were by nature children of wrath, like the rest of mankind. But God, being rich in mercy, because of the great love with which he loved us, even when we were dead in our trespasses, made us alive together with Christ—by grace you have been saved—and raised us up with him and seated us with him in the heavenly places in Christ Jesus.

Even when we were dead in our trespasses...

Do you see how important it was for Paul to make the truth as clear as possible? God interrupted our mess with His mercy.

And as I sing the old familiar hymn...

When I was sinking down,
Sinking down, sinking down,
When I was sinking down,
Sinking down,
When I was sinking down,
Beneath God's righteous frown,
Christ laid aside His crown
For my soul, for my soul,
Christ laid aside His crown
For my soul.

...I can't help but grasp anew at what Paul was trying to get across to his readers, and to us, these centuries later: God's mercy is so extravagant that He stooped down to gently scoop us out of our sin and into His arms.

The moment in which we receive the mercy of God through Christ is the moment He begins to write a new creation chapter in the story of our lives. It is the moment in which a new ring forms to tell a different story of growth in the concentric layers of our journey. God's mercy changes everything because it wasn't activated when we became lovely, lovable, worthy, or wise. His kindness and love aren't extended to the holy, but the humble.

It is in the very nature of our eternal God to extend His mercy to us, His creation, who are otherwise unable to measure up to His holiness. While we were still sinners...even when we were dead...Christ died for us, and brought us back to God the Father. Because of His mercy, because of His love, because of His grace.

God's mercy made the love of God accessible before we could ever even love Him back as He deserves. There is no greater mercy than what God exhibited in Christ. That the Son of God would leave heaven, come to earth, walk among fallen people, be executed as a criminal, and bear the punishment of sin is the supreme demonstration of God's mercy. His mercy made us alive when we were dead, scarred, burnt from the consequences of sin, and unable to turn our lives around. God did it in spite of us. God did it because He is a merciful God. No wonder Betsie ten Boom could say to her sister Corrie even in the very worst state possible, "There is no pit so deep that He is not deeper still."[2]

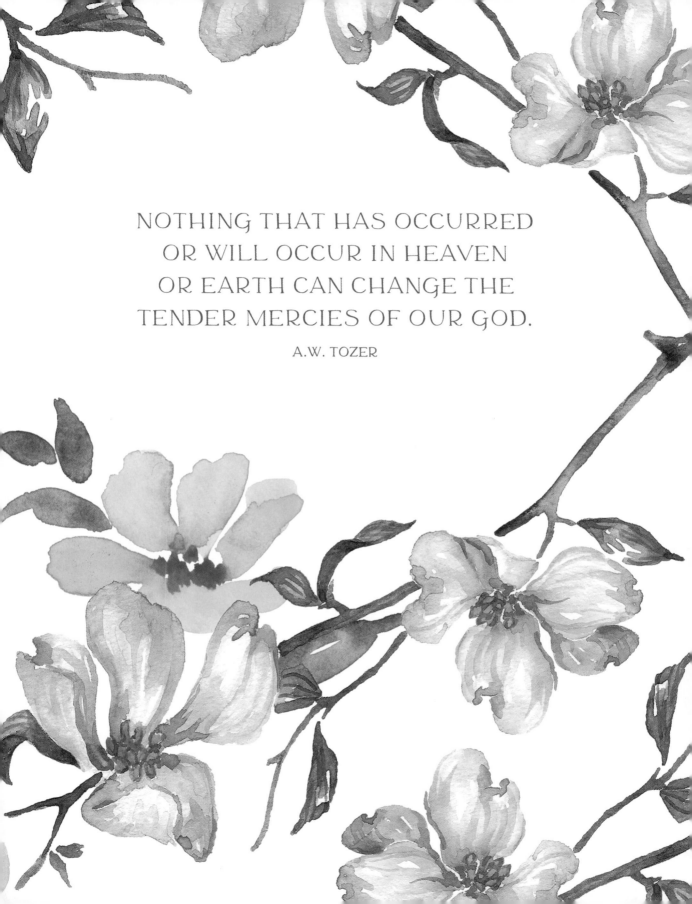

NOTHING THAT HAS OCCURRED
OR WILL OCCUR IN HEAVEN
OR EARTH CAN CHANGE THE
TENDER MERCIES OF OUR GOD.

A.W. TOZER

Friend, do you feel stuck in a pit of regret or shame? Are you tempted to replay the most unlovely parts of your life story again and again in your mind? Our merciful God has extended you the way out, through grace. Receive His extravagant love for you; His mercy is always greater than your sin.

How do we, then, respond to this wondrous love? We start here: The more we set our hearts and minds on the mercy and kindness of God, the more we can't help but offer our lives back to Him in grateful praise as we turn the page from where we've been to where we've always longed to go. If the destination of our pilgrim journey is the presence of God, God's mercy promises to take us there.

GUIDEPOST:

GOD'S MERCY IS ALWAYS GREATER THAN OUR SIN.

Were the whole realm
of nature mine...
Love so amazing,
so divine;
demands my soul,
my life, my all.

4

A DESTINY MADE
SURE BY THE CROSS

If you could snap your fingers and have exactly what you think you need, what would you want to access today...right now? Is it an extended family vacation? Is it a physical body that works, feels, or looks the way you long for it to? Is it success, affirmation, or a promotion that recognizes your hard work? Or perhaps it's close friendships, peace with family members, the hearts of your teen children?

Every one of us is longing for satisfaction. We know that something is missing, so we set out looking to find what we think we need. In many ways, social media seems to be the promised land for satisfaction. For both the consumer and the creator, social media promises happiness, community, affirmation, and the comfort of escapism. But it proves to be a mirage—full of promise, yet disappointingly unsatisfying.

What keeps a generation chasing, on social media, a destination that doesn't truly exist? I think it's the same things that every person of every generation longs for:

> The desire to matter.
> The longing to be loved and noticed.
> The need for community.
> The fear that they'll be forgotten.

CHRIST AS SAVIOR

The word *savior* means "one who saves from danger or destruction." As our Savior, Jesus rescues us from the power and curse of sin. He delivers us from spiritual darkness so that we are no longer children of wrath, but rather, children of light. We who were once separated from God have been restored to fellowship with Him.

The apostle Paul lived two millennia before the rise of social media, but he was driven by these core needs to be satisfied in his achievements. How significant are his words, then, when he writes:

> Indeed, I count everything as loss because of the surpassing worth of knowing Christ Jesus my Lord. For his sake I have suffered the loss of all things and count them as rubbish, in order that I may gain Christ and be found in him, not having a righteousness of my own that comes from the law, but that which comes through faith in Christ, the righteousness from God that depends on faith—that I may know him and the power of his resurrection, and may share his sufferings, becoming like him in his death (Philippians 3:8-10).

Paul didn't share these things with the church at Philippi lightly. He had once known prestige, honor, and the accolades of religious and pious Jews. He had been the best of the best. He had known comfort, luxury, and acceptance. Now, as a transformed and humbled man—serving Christ alone—Paul was hated, imprisoned, beaten, and misunderstood. He was abandoned by trusted friends and often alone. For him to count all else loss compared to the surpassing worth of knowing Christ was a testimony to the greatness of Christ and the gift of redemption through the cross.

The grace and rescue of God won't be satisfying to a person who doesn't realize how hungry he truly is. We won't recognize it at first, but it is a mercy when what we are chasing no longer satisfies.

When we do life's journey without Jesus, we will always find ourselves restless. We will hope, in vain, that once we get over the next hill, beyond the horizon, or reach the peak, we'll feel accomplished and satisfied. But the thrill we're waiting for will never come...because apart from Jesus, it can't.

Indeed, I count everything as loss because of the surpassing worth of knowing Christ Jesus my Lord.

PHILIPPIANS 3:8A

When Jesus said, "I am the bread of life; whoever comes to me shall not hunger, and whoever believes in me shall never thirst" (John 6:35), He wasn't simply soothing a symptom; He was promising the deepest kind of satisfaction. The soul-satisfaction that ends our chasing after empty pursuits.

The deficit and lack that we feel apart from Christ are true representations of our condition before we receive the Bread of Life and the Living Water of redemption in Christ. Our helpless state without Jesus is akin to the sunken-in visage and destitution of starvation and dehydration that occurs when we lack what is needed to sustain us for the journey. In an age of self-exaltation and ambition, we are more helpless, more desperate than we know...or at least than we'll admit.

Nothing we do, acquire, achieve, or perfect can rescue us from the emptiness and destruction our sin and self-reliance lead us to. Only recognizing the emptiness of sin can reveal the satisfaction found in the finished work of Christ on the cross. Only then can we sing,

When I survey the wondrous cross
On which the Prince of glory died,
My richest gain I count but loss,
And pour contempt on all my pride.

Forbid it, Lord, that I should boast,
Save in the death of Christ, my God!
All the vain things that charm me most,
I sacrifice them to His blood.

Because Jesus Christ—the only one who could live a sinless life and fulfill God's plan for restoring fallen people to Himself—died in our place, we who put our trust in Him no longer live for ourselves but for Christ. Through salvation in Christ, we are freed from bondage to sin and self-reliance. We are freed from hoping in the approval, acknowledgment, praise, and adoration of others.

We were made to be satisfied in Jesus. Nothing else will do.

Are you chasing a person, an ambition, or an object of your affection... that will never satisfy? Are you weary, seeking fulfillment where there is no water to quench your thirst?

Hope is ours, friend, because Christ is for us. When Jesus said from the cross, "It is finished," He satisfied every requirement set by His heavenly Father in order to secure our forgiveness, our welcome, our righteousness before a holy God. Because of Christ's finished work, we no longer have to strive to prove ourselves, or chase after earthly gain. With Christ as our Savior, we have a Shepherd who will provide for our every need on the journey. The cross gives us access to every gift the Father offers through His Son. Everything else pales in comparison. Come to Jesus, friend. Only He will satisfy.

GUIDEPOST:

THE CROSS GIVES US ACCESS TO EVERY GIFT THE FATHER OFFERS THROUGH HIS SON.

I AM THE BREAD OF LIFE;

WHOEVER COMES TO ME

SHALL NOT HUNGER,

AND WHOEVER BELIEVES IN

ME SHALL

NEVER THIRST.

JOHN 6:35

No condemnation
now I dread;
Jesus, and
all in Him
is mine!

5

A TRANSFORMATION THAT ENABLES YOU

Have you found yourself wishing you could just be...better?

If only I could run faster, smarter, harder. If only I had more access, more training, more resources. On this journey called life, I'm tempted to think that my biggest problem is what's outside of me, rather than what's inside. If the self-improvement game didn't produce results, we wouldn't be so obsessed with it as a culture. Younger, faster, prettier, healthier, more well-liked, more strategic, and more effective. There's no end to the ways we can try to better ourselves. We can even attempt to defy the aging of our skin with the use of regenerating night creams. (Not to mention all the surgical treatments available to elongate the appearance of youth.) We are a people obsessed with renewal and youth, and so often chase after them at all costs.

It's as if our cultural road signs all flash with the warning, "Be your best self! Forget your past! Remake yourself!"

But in the quiet corners of our lives, we're confronted with the reality that no matter how many serums we use, we can't turn back time. Regardless of how hard we work to be the best version of ourselves right now, we can't change the past. There's a limitation to self-betterment, and we can wear ourselves out trying to achieve a freedom of body, heart, or mind that we cannot acquire through trying harder.

How often do we try to attain something greater than the brokenness of our earthly journeys apart from God? Our constant efforts to fix what ails us come up short and leave us feeling defeated. We were made for much more than improvement, or a little polishing up; we were made for a do-over, a new beginning, a regeneration.

That is why Jesus told Nicodemus in John 3:3, "Truly, I say to you, unless one is born again he cannot see the kingdom of God." Nicodemus was a religious Pharisee, an expert at keeping the law and in perfecting his self-improvement. And yet Jesus made it clear to him: All the looking great on the outside can never get us closer to the heart of God. We must be born again.

Long before Jesus' conversation with Nicodemus, the prophet Ezekiel prophesied how God would restore his people and bring them home from their Babylonian exile:

I will give you a new heart and put a new spirit within you. And I will remove the heart of stone from your flesh and give you a heart of flesh. And I will put my Spirit within you, and cause you to walk in my statutes and be careful to obey my rules (Ezekiel 36:26-27).

These words were for the Jews, God's people, but because God's promises extended to all through Christ, the hope of a new heart is for us too.

You see, before the love of God, through Christ, gets ahold of us and causes us to surrender, the heart is unaware of its deadness. We're unable to have hearts that beat for God, that are supple to His ways and His love for us. A few tweaks

Alive in Him,
my living Head,
and clothed in
righteousness
divine,

Bold I approach the eternal throne, and claim the crown, through Christ, my own.

REGENERATION

This refers to being born again or made new. Regeneration occurs when God imparts spiritual life to us—we are no longer dead in our sins but made alive in Christ. We are given a new heart and a new life. We who were once spiritually blind and unresponsive are enabled to see, understand, and delight in the things of God.

here and there won't break a prisoner's heart free from the shackles of guilt, unworthiness, and sin. It takes the work of the Holy Spirit *in you*, the Father's love *upon you*, and the sacrifice of God's Son, Jesus, *for you*.

Your new heart is straight from the intentional, loving heart of God. And guess what? The new beginning isn't temporary. In case you've forgotten the magnitude of this transformation, let these familiar words stir up a reminder for you:

Long my imprisoned spirit lay
Fast bound in sin and nature's night;
Thine eye diffused a quick'ning ray,
I woke, the dungeon flamed with light.
My chains fell off, my heart was free;
I rose, went forth and followed Thee.

No condemnation now I dread;
Jesus, and all in Him is mine!
Alive in Him, my living Head,
And clothed in righteousness divine;
Bold I approach th'eternal throne
And claim the crown, through Christ, my own.

Remember your new heart, friend...

when you're ready to give up.
when you feel like you're not enough.

when shame and regret creep in.
when you fear what lies ahead.
when it's tempting to keep trying to fix yourself.

Your new heart is made to carry you for the journey Christ has set before you. It's stronger than you think because it's a new heart given by God Himself—not as a result of your attempts at trying harder to make yourself new.

So, weary friend...have you forgotten His promises to make you new from the inside out amidst a world that tells you to preserve all that you can see and touch? We were never meant to be sustained by anything other than a new spiritual heart—one that pumps the new life that courses through our veins because of God's grace.

If you are in Christ, you are born again. You are renewed. You are a new creation. God's divine power has given you everything you need for life and godliness.

When we walk in the reality of this gift, we exercise the muscle of faith. Here, there is no looking back or covering up. Instead, we experience a miracle we couldn't know otherwise: We grow hearts that beat for God. With our new hearts, we have everything we need for the journey.

GUIDEPOST:

WITH OUR NEW HEARTS, WE HAVE EVERYTHING WE NEED FOR THE JOURNEY.

I WILL GIVE YOU A NEW HEART AND PUT A NEW SPIRIT IN YOU. I WILL REMOVE FROM YOU YOUR HEART OF STONE AND GIVE YOU A HEART OF FLESH. AND I WILL PUT MY SPIRIT IN YOU. EZEKIEL 36:26-27A

REPENTANCE IS A
CHANGE OF THE MIND
AND REGENERATION IS
A CHANGE OF THE MAN.

THOMAS ADAMS

Just as I am, Thou wilt receive,
will welcome, pardon, cleanse, relieve;
Because Thy promise I believe,
O Lamb of God, I come, I come!

6

THE RIGHTEOUSNESS
THAT FREES YOU

On a recent adventure into the mountains (as is the weekend routine for the Simons household), we came upon a beautiful lookout point that provided access to the majestic, wooded valley below. We were eager to make our way to the vista point and take in the views. The only problem was that the area had been marred by campers who had built a campfire in the middle of the path and left debris in an otherwise unadulterated area in the woods. We got out of the car, cleaned up the trash, and removed what was left of the campfire that blocked access to the glorious views. The beautiful spot through the trees was restored. It was as if campers had never been there.

If only it were just as easy to remove any trace or evidence of past mistakes or sinful choices in our lives. We can try to cover them up, fix our failures, or shine up our exterior to detract from the mess we've made in areas of our lives. But the truth is that we simply can't erase the effects and consequences of our sin and past mistakes.

But God can. (Deep breath. Pause.)

I don't mean in a trite, feel-good platitude kind of way that makes you feel like you can conquer any mountain with God's help. No, I mean in a surrendered...

Just as I am, without one plea,
But that Thy blood was shed for me,
And that Thou bidd'st me come to Thee,
O Lamb of God, I come, I come!

Just as I am, and waiting not
To rid my soul of one dark blot,
To Thee, whose blood can cleanse each spot,
O Lamb of God, I come, I come!

Just as I am, Thou will receive,
Will welcome, pardon, cleanse, relieve;
Because Thy promise I believe,
O Lamb of God, I come, I come!

...kind of way.

Maybe you've heard it before—the simple definition of justification: Just as if you'd never sinned. It's a catchy way to remember the meaning of an otherwise transactional word. But friend, it's so much more than even that. We are justified and invited to come and draw near, just as we are. The wonder of God's gift of grace through Jesus is that God declares us righteous when we trust in the sacrificial death and resurrection of Jesus Christ, the perfect Son of God who lived a sinless life and paid the price for *our* sin. Just as I am...I have no way to fix my past. Just as I am...I can't erase the wrongs I've done or wrongs that have been done to me. Just as I am...I can't restore what's been broken.

But just as we are...when we come to Jesus and trust in Him, we are covered by His righteousness, and therefore, made right with God. Does that rub you the wrong way like it does me at times? Just as I am? Don't I need to clean myself up or get my act together

GOD DOES NOT JUSTIFY US
BECAUSE WE ARE WORTHY,
BUT JUSTIFYING MAKES US WORTHY.

THOMAS WATSON

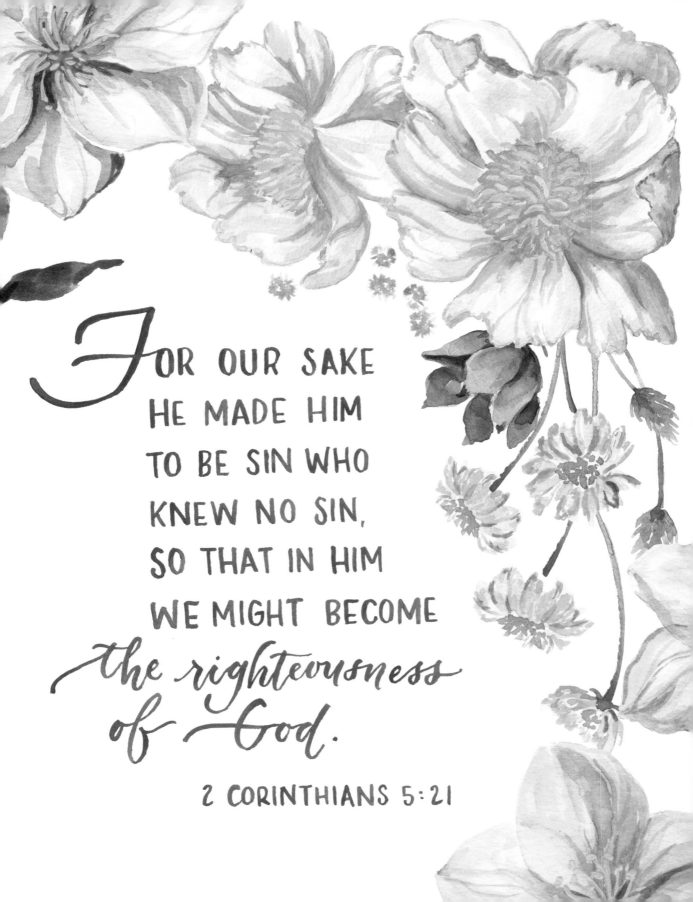

For our sake
he made him
to be sin who
knew no sin,
so that in him
we might become
the righteousness
of God.

2 CORINTHIANS 5:21

first? The truth is, our pride so often keeps us from approaching God because we would rather come with all our good intentions, efforts, and perfected strategies...rather than coming to God as weak, worn, foolish, and frail.

We come to Jesus fully surrendered, or we don't truly come at all. We can't receive the gift of God's justification if we don't come recognizing we need it in the first place. But when we come, He offers true freedom and substitution for all our insufficiencies. When we trust in Jesus, God no longer sees the sum of our mistakes, poor choices, secret sins, or the foolishness of our self-reliance.

As if we had never sinned. The eternal consequences due us are removed and cast away.

The good news isn't simply that we no longer stand marred, scarred, shamed, and unworthy; it's that we are made new, whole, righteous, and worthy because of Jesus' worthiness. In 2 Corinthians 5:21, the apostle Paul describes it this way: "For our sake he made him to be sin who knew no sin, so that in him we might become the righteousness of God."

You see, justification is not simply absolution as if we had never sinned, but God's favor as if we had always been righteous. When He looks at you, He sees the righteousness of Christ. Does that blow your mind? It should!

God erases the eternal consequences of our sin, not by turning away from His justice, but by upholding His justice. It's as if God Himself stooped low, picked up the trash with His bare hands, and cleared away the debris from the mess we left behind. It's as if He had not only removed any trace that mars the pristine spot in the woods, making it accessible and restored, but planted a new grove of pines as well. He doesn't just remove the mark of sin; He remakes with the mark of righteousness. As one Puritan noted, "God does not justify us because we are worthy, but justifying makes us worthy."[3]

Friend, we are not yet sinless on this side of heaven. But we can know true freedom from the burden of sin because the blood of Jesus covers and justifies us. How? Perhaps

JUSTIFICATION

When we receive Christ as Savior, our sins are forgiven, Christ's righteousness is given to us, and we are declared "not guilty." Christ's shed blood on the cross was the ransom payment that frees us from enslavement to sin and makes us right before God. Having been justified, our sins are no longer counted against us, and we now have access to God—forever.

we've forgotten the benefits of His grace through justification. Consider what Paul recounts in Romans 5:1-11. Look carefully for the promises in this description.

> Therefore, since we have been justified by faith, we have peace with God through our Lord Jesus Christ. Through him we have also obtained access by faith into this grace in which we stand, and we rejoice in hope of the glory of God. Not only that, but we rejoice in our sufferings, knowing that suffering produces endurance, and endurance produces character, and character produces hope, and hope does not put us to shame, because God's love has been poured into our hearts through the Holy Spirit who has been given to us.

> For while we were still weak, at the right time Christ died for the ungodly. For one will scarcely die for a righteous person—though perhaps for a good person one would dare even to die—but God shows his love for us in that while we were still sinners, Christ died for us. Since, therefore, we have now been justified by his blood, much more shall we be saved by him from the wrath of God. For if while we were enemies we were reconciled to God by the death of his Son, much more, now that we are reconciled, shall we be saved by his life. More than that, we also rejoice in God through our Lord Jesus Christ, through whom we have now received reconciliation.

We are promised...

peace with God (verse 1)
access to grace (verse 2)
hope in the glory of God (verse 2b)
rejoicing in suffering that produces endurance (verses 3-4)

hope and the love of God (verse 5)
salvation from God's wrath (verse 9)
reconciliation to God (verse 10)
joy in God (verse 11)

We may not yet know sinlessness, but because of Jesus, we have access to all of this because we've been justified. How generous is our God? He doesn't just fix; He restores.

How might you live this day differently knowing you are made worthy because of the righteousness of Christ? How might the guidepost of God's grace through making us right with Him change the course of your thoughts, your actions, and your path ahead?

When we see ourselves as God sees us, through the lens of grace, we will realize we no longer need to make ourselves right through attempts at worthiness. We can walk in righteousness because God has made us right with Him.

GUIDEPOST:

WE CAN WALK IN RIGHTEOUSNESS BECAUSE GOD HAS MADE US RIGHTEOUS.

He leadeth me,
O blessed thought!
O words with
heavenly comfort
fraught!
Whate'er I do,
whate'er I be,
still 'tis God's
hand that leadeth
me.

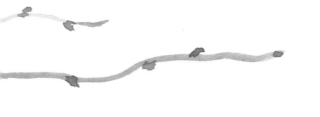

7

HIS EVER-WATCHFUL CARE

I f I could have one superpower, I'd probably choose to be all-knowing. (I know—that doesn't seem quite as exciting as having the power to make chips and queso calories disappear, does it?) I suppose if I'm being honest here, the desire to know the future, the outcome, or the way it will all play out betrays the real issue in the natural state of my heart: I trust in myself and my ability to orchestrate the outcomes I desire.

*If I only knew...*I could avoid pain, disappointment, failure, loss. Navigating life's journey can be fearful for the one who relies on herself to know the way...but doesn't.

I recently read about a rigorous test aspiring taxi drivers in London must pass if they hope to earn a coveted "green badge" and become certified to drive one of London's iconic black taxi cabs. The test is called the Knowledge, and it requires drivers to be virtually omniscient about the 25,000 hard-to-navigate streets within a six-mile radius of the city's center, not to mention landmarks, tourist attractions, restaurants, and businesses within the area. Students prepare for years to take this test—dedicating innumerable hours studying and learning the best and fastest routes, acquiring everything there is to know about the convoluted, disorienting streets of London—knowledge no GPS could provide.

How might you feel stepping into one of London's famous black taxi cabs knowing the driver's near-impossible-to-fathom knowledge of every street in the heart of London? I imagine you'd be relieved to know your arrival at your destination was in the hands of someone who didn't simply rely on a GPS or ride-share app map, but on knowledge he knew by heart.

So often, as Christ-followers, we feel as if we are navigating our way through life fumbling with a map that's not up to date, when we're actually led and directed by a God who knows all things. We fret and find ourselves overwhelmed when we can't think ourselves into the answers to our questions:

What happens if I get sick and can't keep up with my job?
Where should we raise our family?
Will I get married? When?
How do I choose the right career?
What if I miss my calling?
Who should I pursue to be my friend?
What will I do when my kids are out of the house?
Will I ever feel like I belong?

These and so many other questions swirl in our minds, dangling the promise of a satisfactory answer if we could just *know more, understand better, see into the future.* Our worries tempt us to play master of our own lives rather than depend on the Master whose omniscience can point us in the right direction.

O Lord, You have searched me and known me!

YOU KNOW WHEN I SIT DOWN
AND WHEN I RISE UP;

YOU DISCERN MY
THOUGHTS FROM AFAR.

YOU SEARCH OUT MY PATH
AND MY LYING DOWN

AND ARE ACQUAINTED
WITH ALL MY WAYS.

PSALM 139:1-3

THE OMNISCIENCE OF GOD

God knows all things both actual and possible. His knowledge is perfect and complete—He knows the past, present, and future, as well as our hearts. He knows every single one of our struggles, burdens, and needs, and watches over us with great care at all times.

We were never meant to be all-knowing and all-wise, but some of us wear ourselves out trying to get there.

The psalmist, David, shows us the posture we're meant to have, instead, in Psalm 139:1-6:

> O Lord, you have searched me and known me!
> You know when I sit down and when I rise up;
>   you discern my thoughts from afar.
> You search out my path and my lying down
>   and are acquainted with all my ways.
> Even before a word is on my tongue,
>   behold, O Lord, you know it altogether.
> You hem me in, behind and before,
>   and lay your hand upon me.
> Such knowledge is too wonderful for me;
>   it is high; I cannot attain it.

The Old Testament Hebrew word for "searched" in verse 1 means to excavate, to examine carefully, to penetrate beneath the surface. God sees beyond our facades and lip service. He knows what's going on in our hearts. And so, the word for "known" here is not merely factual or informational. Instead, it carries the idea of seeing clearly, or to know intimately. David rightly described God's omniscience as personal and inescapable. He was vulnerable and exposed to a holy God who knew all his ways, and yet he felt safe. Why? Because

he knew God's character. David realized that God not only knew about his every move and every thought, but truly cared for him.

Believing God according to His character changes the way we think about our lives—past, present, and future. I love how Timothy Keller puts it: "God will only give you what you would have asked for if you knew everything he knows."[4]

God knows us better than we know ourselves. He knows the fears we hide, the questions we're sometimes too afraid to ask, and the worries that keep us up at night. He is well acquainted with our innermost thoughts and our deepest longings. The psalmist does not describe God's knowledge and omniscience as scrutinizing and shaming, but as displaying intimacy, tenderness, and care. His omniscience doesn't cast us out, but brings us near.

This is the omniscient God who said through the prophet Isaiah,

> I am God, and there is none like me, declaring the end from the beginning and from ancient times things not yet done, saying, "My counsel shall stand, and I will accomplish all my purpose" (Isaiah 46:9-10).

You see, we don't have to have all the answers to the big and small questions we face every day; we need only follow an all-knowing God.

Because of God's omniscience...

> He knows our thoughts (Psalm 139:2).
> He understands us (Psalm 139:1-6).
> He leads us through our struggles (Psalm 23:4-6).
> He works all things together for our good (Romans 8:28).
> Our future is secure (Romans 8:29-30).

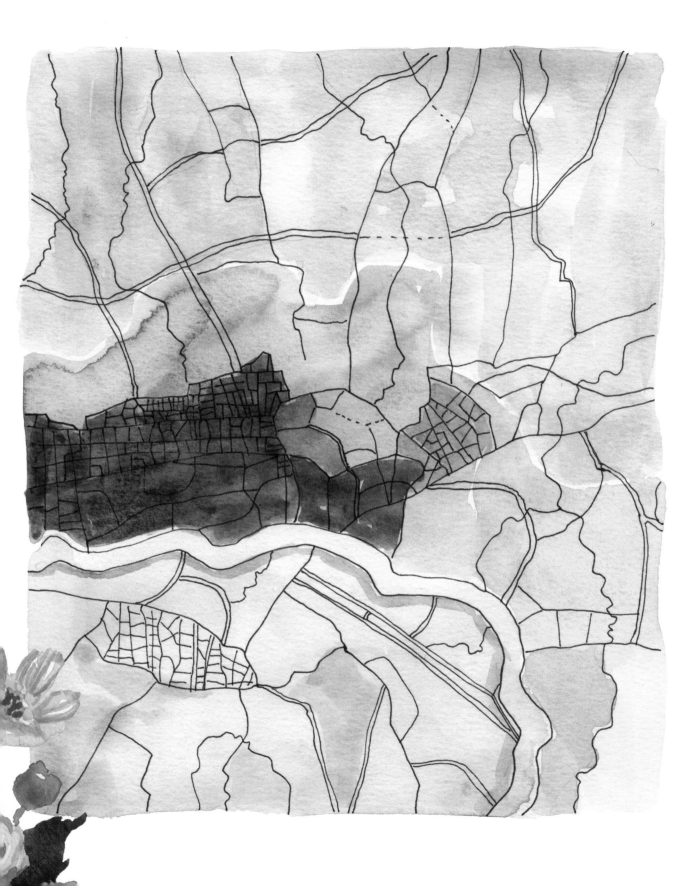

He knows all our needs and will supply them (Matthew 6:25-32).
Nothing takes Him by surprise (Psalm 139:16).
Justice belongs to Him (Proverbs 15:3).
Nothing is impossible for Him (Psalm 147:5).

Does that comfort you as it does me? We serve a God who knows infinitely more than landmarks, locations, or perfectly timed routes through 25,000 windy, crooked London streets. Because God sees all and knows all, we can trust where He takes us...with His wisdom and power. When we allow Him to direct our steps (or "take the wheel," shall we say?), we realign our hearts with the character of God and rest in the fact that He knows all things. And when this is the posture of our hearts, we can't help but sing:

He leadeth me, O blessed thought!
O words with heavenly comfort fraught!
Whate'er I do, where'er I be,
still 'tis God's hand that leadeth me.

We have nothing to fear and no reason to fret, for we are in the hands of a Maker who knows what we need.

GUIDEPOST:

BECAUSE GOD SEES ALL AND KNOWS ALL, WE CAN TRUST WHERE HE TAKES US.

ABIDE WITH ME!
FAST FALLS THE EVENTIDE

THE DARKNESS DEEPENS;
LORD, WITH ME ABIDE
WHEN OTHER HELPERS
FAIL AND COMFORTS FLEE,
HELP OF THE HELPLESS,
OH, ABIDE WITH ME!

8

NEVER ALONE

Most summer nights, you can find me hanging around a campfire with my six sons and my mountain-man husband. We live just minutes away from a wooded canyon here in Western Colorado. Sometimes we bring brats to grill, and if we do, we certainly bring along s'mores makings as well. The wood and kindling are gathered, and we get to work. Like a riotous dance, the flames and smoke first put on their dramatic show before quieting to the warmth and crackle of campfire embers. Even the warmest summer's night turns crisp after the sun goes down when you're in the deep of the canyon. So we gather 'round with jackets and blankets, and let the smoke of the fire engulf us. Sooner or later, we notice the time—and because we live just minutes away, we pack up and head home to sleep in our own beds. Folding chairs are put away, all the food returns to the cooler, the boys make sure the fire is out, and we leave the site the way we found it.

As you know, a funny thing happens when you return home from a night around a campfire: There is no mistaking where you've been. Every piece of clothing on your body—and even your hair—smells of the campfire smoke. Smoke isn't bound by location and it isn't something you wipe away; it permeates everything and leaves nothing untouched. Long after the last ember cools, the effects of that fire continue to stay with you, wherever you go.

THE OMNIPRESENCE OF GOD

God is fully everywhere at all times. This gives us the assurance that we are never out of His presence. Not only is God everywhere, but He is with us every place we go. How comforting it is to know we can count on His presence at every moment in our lives!

I think of David's words in Psalm 139, just following the ones about God's intimate knowledge of him. He confesses and acknowledges this to the Lord:

Where shall I go from your Spirit?
 Or where shall I flee from your presence?
If I ascend to heaven, you are there!
 If I make my bed in Sheol, you are there!
If I take the wings of the morning
 and dwell in the uttermost parts of the sea,
even there your hand shall lead me,
 and your right hand shall hold me (verses 7-10).

Unlike a god of our making that sits idly on a shelf or as an idol in our hearts, the God of the Bible is not bound by time or space, location or limits. The Lord our God is omnipresent. He is in all places at all times.

It should feel unfathomable to our finite minds that God could be everywhere all at once. Isn't it beyond comprehension? It is! That God is simultaneously in the Northern and Southern Hemispheres. That He hears the prayers of a weary mom in Colorado while He attends to the prayers of a frustrated father in Maine. That He is present when we're at church...and when we hide away in our sin.

What's overwhelming and beyond comprehension isn't simply that He is an omnipresent God; it's that He chooses to be everywhere we are, even when we don't choose to be with Him. As the Puritan writer William Secker observed, "A man may hide God from himself, and yet he cannot hide himself from God."[5]

God is our
refuge and
strength,
an ever-present
help in trouble.

PSALM 46:1

You see, God's omnipresence is dreadful to the one who fears His presence; but for the one who knows Him to be merciful, loving, faithful, and good, His omnipresence assures and comforts.

Is He there when my child is in the hospital? He is.

Is He near when I've been hurt by a friend? He is.

Is He there when I feel all alone? He is.

Is He present when I've made a mess of my circumstances? He is.

Is He with me when I'm facing the darkest of times? He is.

Is He there when I need a second chance? He is.

> I am sure that neither death nor life, nor angels nor rulers, nor things present nor things to come, nor powers, nor height nor depth, nor anything else in all creation, will be able to separate us from the love of God in Christ Jesus our Lord (Romans 8:38-39).

God is not just everywhere; He is where you *are*.

> As a mom to six, I'm always declaring, "Wait, boys! I'm one person, I can't be in two places at the same time!" But God...He can. He doesn't ask us to wait because He's unavailable. He is not an absent Father. To be unbound by time and space is in God's very nature, and therefore, it is impossible for Him to miss a single detail. He is never too busy someplace else to attend to your needs in the here and now. Isn't that the most comforting truth? God not only sees the challenges and heartaches you are walking through today; He is with you.

Abide with me! Fast falls the eventide.

The familiar hymn continues...

> *The darkness deepens; Lord, with me abide!*
> *When other helpers fail and comforts flee,*
> *Help of the helpless, oh, abide with me!*

What a contrast to the fleeting and fickle things of this world—quickly disappearing when the warmth of the fire goes out. But not our God. He remains and stays. He moves in, takes over, leaves nothing untouched. He isn't far off, but near. He isn't distracted, but present. It's in the most difficult points of our journeys that we realize God is the only one who has always been with us.

So let it be your confidence and assurance, pilgrim: "God is our refuge and strength, an ever-present help in trouble" (Psalm 46:1 NIV).

No matter where we are, God is with us and will never leave us. We do not walk alone. We can't lose our way from His presence when He always knows His way to us.

GUIDEPOST:

NO MATTER WHERE WE ARE, GOD IS WITH US AND WILL NEVER LEAVE US.

I WILL NEVER
LEAVE YOU
NOR FORSAKE YOU.

HEBREWS 13:5

When darkness seems to hide his face,
I rest on his unchanging grace;
In every high and stormy gale,
my anchor holds within the veil.

ON CHRIST THE SOLID ROCK
I STAND; ALL OTHER GROUND
IS SINKING SAND.

9

A SURE AND STEADFAST GUIDE

Do you crave stability, friend? I don't mean predictability, per se, but real stability and assurance? *Me too.* I see you... trying to make sure your family's health and well-being are secure. I see you...working to give your kids a solid foundation of faith. I see you...seeking to have reliability in your resources and finances. I'm there too, trying to find sure footing in a sea of unknowns.

When we're confident in our circumstances, relationships, and responsibilities, we thrive and step forward with courage. But just the opposite is true as well. In the same way that crossing a river on a handful of loosely anchored rocks feels risky and unsure, we question every step when we're not anchored securely to solid ground.

I've lived just north of the Golden Gate Bridge in San Francisco twice, and during both seasons, I traversed this iconic suspension bridge almost weekly, marveling at its magnificent beauty and impressive engineering. Every day, more than 110,000 vehicles cross the bridge without their drivers questioning the stability of its 8,981-foot span from end to end across the waters of the San Francisco

Bay. Bridges like the Golden Gate are anchored deeply into the bedrock below the water (for the Golden Gate, that's 65 feet and more underground); they must be if they are to withstand high winds, raging storms, and crashing waves. For any structure to be truly stable, it must be anchored to solid ground.

This is why it matters, on life's journey, that we not simply grasp at temporary buoys. It's not enough to just hold on to something, we need to pay attention to the permanence of what, or Who, we cling to.

If there is one attribute of God that is difficult to comprehend, it is that God never changes. How do we wrap our minds around an idea so beyond our everyday reality and understanding? Everything about human existence is about change. We grow; God doesn't. We have faults; He is sinless. We improve; He doesn't. We are fickle; He remains the same.

We seek change—with homes, jobs, friends, communities, leaders, diets, churches, locations, identities, and more—because we are longing for our ideal, our desire for better, truer, more stable, a sense of perfection. We want to sink our lives into something that won't leave us disappointed. So we keep running, keep searching, keep trying to fix, improve, and reinvent. In a world that is constantly changing its mind and declaring no absolutes, we find ourselves longing to anchor our lives to something—or someone—real.

So when God reveals Himself as the Beginning and the End, the one who cannot and will not change, fade, evolve, or go back on His word, we hesitate and wonder: Can I really trust Him?

God is permanent and immovable:
Of old you laid the foundation of the earth,
and the heavens are the work of your hands.

THE BELIEVING MAN
ACCEPTS A PROMISE
OF GOD AS A FACT
AS SOLID AS
A MOUNTAIN AND
VASTLY MORE
ENDURING.

A.W. TOZER

THE IMMUTABILITY OF GOD

God is perfectly unchanging—He is eternally steadfast and faithful. This means He is forever trustworthy, and His character is dependable. We can rest assured that God will always be consistent in His every interaction with us—His love and care for us will never diminish.

They will perish, but you will remain;
> they will all wear out like a garment.
You will change them like a robe, and they will pass away,
> but you are the same, and your years have no end (Psalm 102:25-27).

The psalmist recognized that God, as the author and creator of all things, is permanent, unchanging, and is not searching for better, like we are. He *is* the ideal. He *is* truth. He *is* perfection. He *is* the real anchor we can rely on. Because God exists as the unchanging center of all creation, we needn't endlessly search for a better way when we journey with our strong, changeless, immutable God.

God's purposes are unchanging:

Remember this and stand firm,
> recall it to mind, you transgressors,
> remember the former things of old;
for I am God, and there is no other;
> I am God, and there is none like me,
declaring the end from the beginning
> and from ancient times things not yet done,
saying, "My counsel shall stand,
> and I will accomplish all my purpose" (Isaiah 46:8-10).

God's promises are fulfilled:

> God is not man, that he should lie, or a son of man, that he should change his mind. Has he said, and will not do it? Or has he spoken, and will he not fulfill it? (Numbers 23:19).

God does not take back His gifts:

> The gifts and the calling of God are irrevocable (Romans 11:29).

Do you see it? God is not capricious. He is not susceptible to mood swings and does not get flustered. His immutability means that we can trust who He is, what He has done, and what He promises to do.

Some of us have journeyed far too long believing that we alone must be the rock of stability and reliability—for ourselves and for everyone else. How exhausting it is when we attempt to be the source of permanence and perfection that we were never meant to be.

Others of us have chased paths we hope will lead us to greater security and happiness, only to find that nothing on earth can still our wandering minds...no one can settle our restless hearts.

But God.

Only a holy, unchanging, immutable God is worthy of echoing this old and familiar melody:

> *When darkness seems to hide his face,*
> *I rest on his unchanging grace;*
> *In every high and stormy gale,*
> *My anchor holds within the veil.*
> *On Christ the solid rock I stand;*
> *all other ground is sinking sand;*
> *all other ground is sinking sand.*

We have this as a sure and steadfast anchor of the soul, a hope that enters into the inner place behind the curtain, where Jesus has gone as a forerunner on our behalf

HEBREWS 6:19-20

As Hebrews 6:19-20 says, "We have this as a sure and steadfast anchor of the soul, a hope that enters into the inner place behind the curtain, where Jesus has gone as a forerunner on our behalf, having become a high priest forever after the order of Melchizedek."

Simply put, as Christ-followers, Jesus is now our only way to access the holy God of the universe. We are anchored to a sure and steady Father because of the redeeming grace of God, not because of any good we have done. Through Jesus, we are anchored to a sure and unchanging Father, even as we ourselves are fickle and faithless.

So, let us hold fast to our unchanging, immutable God. He is immovable, unshakeable, undeterred. He cannot lie, and He does not go back on His word. "Every good gift and every perfect gift is from above, coming down from the Father of lights, with whom there is no variation or shadow due to change" (James 1:17). When we rest in Him, we put our trust in the surest and steadiest of anchors.

GUIDEPOST:

THROUGH JESUS, WE ARE ANCHORED TO A SURE AND UNCHANGING FATHER.

A LONG ENDURANCE

It is always hard to see the purpose in
wilderness wanderings until after they are over.

John Bunyan,
The Pilgrim's Progress

I NEED THEE EVERY HOUR

10
EVERY NEED ALWAYS SUPPLIED

Farmers need rain, rivers need melting snow, and the earth needs its exact gravitational constant in order to operate as God intended it to. To be dependent is exactly how God created all of creation, and yet at times it seems that *need* is a welcomed reality everywhere but in the human heart. I don't know about you, but I struggle to have need, to be dependent, to *not* be enough for everything I have on my plate. I'd love to believe it when I'm told that I need no one but myself in order to be happy, but I know better. My heart knows the truth: I'm not enough. I have need, and that's the way it ought to be.

Even those whom God used in mighty ways had needs, great and small: Moses needed passage to the Promised Land. Abraham needed God to do the impossible to make him a father. Jonah needed compassion. Peter needed faith. Paul needed an awakening. And Mary, the mother of Jesus, needed a place to deliver her baby. None of them could accomplish, on their own, what God had called them to without dependence on His provision. There isn't one believer, past or present, who hasn't felt they were lacking in some area of their life—in visible or invisible ways.

THE PROVISION OF GOD

God preserves and cares for His creation. He is intimately involved in our lives and sustains us. Under His care, every need we have will be met. Every provision we enjoy in life comes from Him alone and reflects His faithfulness to us and His love for us.

Houses,
  friends,
  a job promotion.

  Money in the bank,
    food on the table,
    a church to call home.

A sense of peace,
      a shoulder to cry on,
        wisdom for the problems we can't fix.

Though we are obsessed with relying on ourselves, the unpopular truth remains: We are desperate, lacking, and unable to be our own source for all the things we need. We simply can't provide for ourselves.

In Southwestern Colorado, where the terrain is mountainous and the ground often hard and unfertile, I try to grow things. But without tremendous mending, the soil simply can't provide for the crops or flower beds I long to see. I need nutrients for the soil, rain to fall, and the sun to do its work; I can't simply cause seeds to spring up into new growth. In spite of any and all efforts of a wannabe gardener, it's the providence of God that determines yield. The same can be said of life's journey.

We are equally wannabe master gardeners of our own lives. The native soil from which we try to provide for all that our hearts need is far from

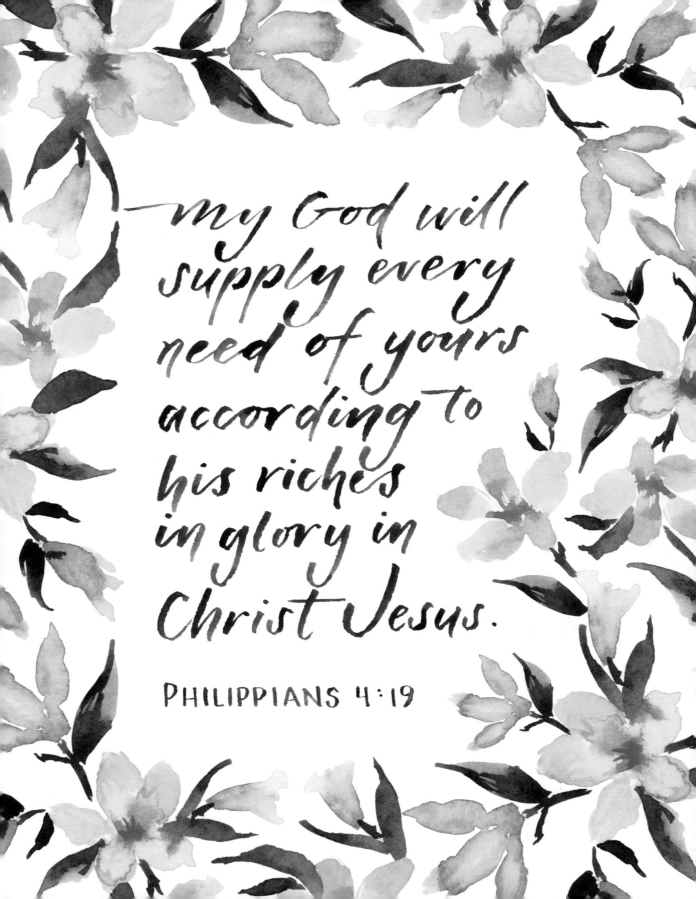

my God will supply every need of yours according to his riches in glory in Christ Jesus.

PHILIPPIANS 4:19

sufficient. It's not even close to being capable of supplying what you and I truly need. But in our stubbornness and pride, we keep trying—working harder and harder in hopes of finding fulfillment, satisfaction, and all that we need.

The root word from which we get the term *providence* means "to see beforehand, a prior seeing, a foresight," but it encompasses so much more than just foreknowledge. Providence carries the idea of guardianship and care...a preparation for the future. Simply put, providence means that God will take care of us; He is our provision.

Paul speaks of this provision in Philippians 4:19: "My God will supply every need of yours according to his riches in glory in Christ Jesus." What does he mean? What can we learn about God's provision through Paul's description? I'm getting a bit word nerdy here today, but the meaning of *supply*, in the original Greek text, means "to fulfill, fill to the brim, render complete, fully execute, bring to realization." Sounds a lot like providence, right?

What a promise: God will bring your every need to fulfillment, to satisfaction...to completion. You must be wondering how this is true, considering how long you've waited for God to provide for that request that comes up every time you speak with Him. Well, the beauty of God's word is that His promises don't stand alone or in contradiction to any of His whole counsel. And so, when you consider your great needs and how God meets them, you'll realize how important it is to understand this promise in light of the context Paul gives next in this profound verse: "according to his riches in glory in Christ Jesus." *Wow.*

Paul wants you to know that there are no bounds to God's provision. He meets every possible need first and foremost through bringing you back to Himself through Jesus. God can and will provide for your health, finances, shelter, nourishment, relationships, pain, fears, and dreams. He can and will complete the good work He began in you (Philippians 1:6), but He will also "make all grace abound to you, so that having all sufficiency in all things at all times, you may abound in every good work" (2 Corinthians 9:8).

But our access to His providential care and provision is through Christ, and Christ meets our greatest spiritual need for communion with God. Without the latter, we could never truly experience the former.

Physical need, financial need, emotional need, spiritual need—not one is fully met through earthly means alone; they are first and foremost satisfied through the gift of grace through Christ. We were meant to receive restoration through Christ as God's greatest provision. Every other need finds its source in the one who meets our greatest need to be made whole in Him.

Charles Spurgeon says it better: "I have a great need for Christ; I have a great Christ for my need."[6]

Christ transforms our native soil so that we might know the providential care of a good God—a God who doesn't just foresee all times and all things, but meets us in our need in the midst of everything He purposes.

God promises to meet our every need. So let the following be our prayer, that we might rejoice in our needs as opportunities to discover God's providence and provision. May we be quick to desire His fullness and supply as we trust in His promises:

I need Thee ev'ry hour,
Teach me Thy will;
And Thy rich promises
In me fulfill.

Let it be, Lord. Let us need You now and find You faithful—always.

— GUIDEPOST: —

GOD PROMISES TO MEET OUR EVERY NEED.

I have a great need for Christ; I have a great Christ for my need.

C.H. SPURGEON

AND GOD IS ABLE TO
BLESS YOU ABUNDANTLY,
SO THAT IN ALL THINGS
AT ALL TIMES, HAVING ALL
THAT YOU NEED,
YOU WILL ABOUND IN
EVERY GOOD WORK.

2 CORINTHIANS 9:8

PRAISE GOD, FROM WHOM

ALL BLESSINGS FLOW;

PRAISE HIM, ALL

CREATURES HERE BELOW.

PRAISE HIM ABOVE,

YE HEAV'NLY HOST;

PRAISE FATHER, SON

AND HOLY GHOST.

11

BLESSINGS WITHOUT END

My boys love to fish the rivers that form the headwaters of the Rio Grande, high up in the mountains near the Continental Divide in the San Juan Mountains. Up at that elevation, you can often find snow still melting in the summer months, feeding into the rivers that become the Rio Grande, which flows down through Colorado, then New Mexico, and ends in Chihuahua, Mexico. Standing at the river's edge with my boys last summer, I imagined the journey these waters take as they wind through mountains and valleys. Along the way, they irrigate the desert of central New Mexico and pass by historic pueblos and dwellings, then continue on to the border between the US and Mexico.

So many people count on this river to irrigate their lands and to feed their people. From the remote silence of a fishing hole tucked into a mountain's side, I marvel: This is where it all begins. The desert communities to the south of Colorado are dependent on the snowmelt and rainfall that gather at the headwaters. The more moisture the Rio Grande

THE GOODNESS OF GOD

Everything that God does is perfectly good and emanates out of His goodness—including His justice and discipline. We can be confident that in every way possible He is good to us, even when we cannot understand how it is so. He delights in blessing us, and His plans and will for us always have our ultimate good in mind.

receives, the more the communities benefit from its abundance. Some years, the Rio Grande flows to a trickle, and during droughts, the desert seems to swallow up what remains of the water. Those who rely on the river are at the mercy of the headwaters to supply their needs.

This reminds me of how many times I've been tempted to worry about supply in my journey with Christ. So often, I've allowed myself to believe the river of His grace might run out as I am walking in the desert. How easy it is to doubt the strength of the flow when we forget who is at the source.

The headwaters for any blessing, any provision, any resource for our journey is God Himself. But that in itself means very little unless you know the character of God, right? How can any traveler rely on a map unless he trusts the cartographer? Do we eat food offered to us from a stranger? We're instructed from the earliest age to be suspicious. The source matters. When we don't know who it is that supplies, we can't fully trust the provision.

So who is this God who supplies our needs? He is a good God:

> Oh, taste and see that the LORD is good! Blessed is the man who takes refuge in him! (Psalm 34:8).

As we walk the parched paths and stony passes in life, we can trust God's character and know that He will provide true refuge for our weary hearts. Yes, God can get us out of a sticky situation, and He has the power to change our circumstances, but we could not trust Him or find shelter in Him if not for His goodness.

Because God is good, everything that flows from Him must be good as well. In Psalm 31:19, David wrote, "Oh, how abundant is your goodness, which

Oh, taste
and see
that the Lord
is good!
Blessed
is the man
who takes
refuge in
Him!

PSALM 34:8

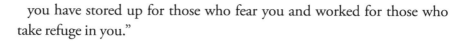

you have stored up for those who fear you and worked for those who take refuge in you."

God's goodness isn't simply that He is nice, kind, or helpful; God's goodness is the nonnegotiable standard of beauty, virtue, and wholesomeness that He embodies. God doesn't have to try to be good; He simply is good. Let that truly sink in and flood you with the relief you've been longing for. You and I belong to a God who is trustworthy because everything He does emanates from His goodness.

Praise God, from whom all blessings flow;
Praise Him, all creatures here below.
Praise Him above, ye heav'nly host;
Praise Father, Son and Holy Ghost.

The first lines of the Doxology are what come to mind when I read Paul's words in Romans 11:36: "From him and through him and to him are all things. To him be glory forever." God's goodness to us will never run dry. From whom all blessings flow. He's the headwaters that never run dry.

Take a deep breath, and rest. You and I don't have to muster up for ourselves all that God promises to supply out of His goodness. He is a good Father, and we're called to receive the blessings that come from Him.

Because of God's goodness...

He is the source of every one of our blessings (James 1:17).
He sustains our lives (Matthew 6:25-34).
He supplies our every need (Philippians 4:19).

How might we see our days differently if we were to consider God's goodness continually? Would we be so quick to doubt His plans? Would we fret about our circumstances? Would we get anxious over not-yet-answered prayers?

The steadiness by which we walk secure in our journeys with Christ has everything to do with our confidence in the character of God.

We too readily think of God's good for us according to our standards, trying to fit Him into a box of our understanding. But how frightful and wearying it is to navigate life's mountains and valleys according to our own understanding of good. Instead, when we understand God to be true goodness and His very character to be good, we begin to see how "for those who love God all things work together for good, for those who are called according to his purpose" (Romans 8:28).

When we realize that God Himself is the definition of goodness, then we see how all that is true of His character—His sovereignty, omnipotence, and goodness—works in unison. If God is the very essence of goodness in our lives, we will have the good we seek, because in receiving God's greatest provision, we will have Christ.

It is not enough that we acknowledge God's infinite resources; we must believe also that he is infinitely generous to bestow them.[7]

A.W. Tozer

GUIDEPOST:

GOD'S GOODNESS TO US WILL NEVER RUN DRY.

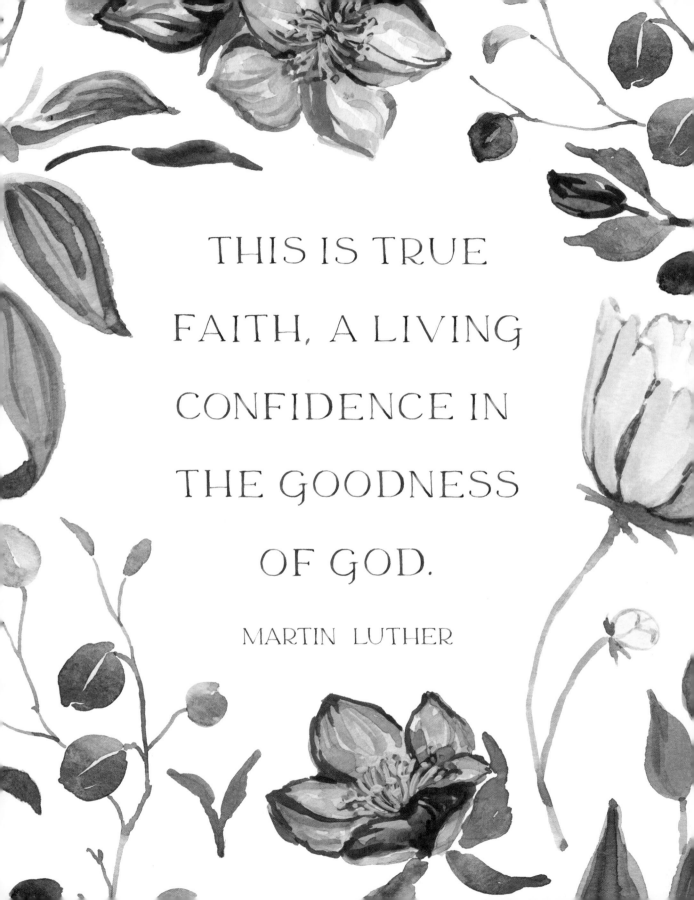

THIS IS TRUE
FAITH, A LIVING
CONFIDENCE IN
THE GOODNESS
OF GOD.

MARTIN LUTHER

I know not the
way He leads me,
but well do I
know my Guide.

12

AT YOUR SIDE...
ALL THE WAY
HOME

For all the busyness that marks modern life, we seem to be living in days when people don't actually know where they're going. Aimless—lacking direction or purpose—feels more accurate a description for the journey so many are on. I can't help but wonder: Have we made such entertainment out of following others that we've lost sight of what we're aiming for? It may not be obvious in the everydayness of life, but we are led, directed, influenced—even *discipled*—every time we pick up our smartphones.

I don't have to tell you, but we live in a world obsessed with influencing, leading, and acquiring followers—always seeking new and better ways to convince others we ought to be the ones out in front. But at the same time, most of us are blindly following, not even realizing how influenced we truly are. As our devices consume more and more of our lives, following someone has become more than the tap of a button; it is more akin to subscribing to a form of discipleship. In this current landscape of people mindlessly allowing others to daily shape how they think, feel, and see the world, I can't help but have a whole

CHRIST AS SHEPHERD

As our Great Shepherd, Jesus watches over, protects, and provides for us. His every action toward us is filled with tenderness and compassion; in Him, all our needs are met. His devotion to us is total, and with Him at our side, we have nothing to fear. There is no greater companion we could ask for in life's journey.

new appreciation for Jesus' description of us, His children. He calls us sheep.

> Sheep are defenseless.
> Sheep follow mindlessly, wander aimlessly.
> Sheep have no sense of direction.

Is it any wonder that Jesus speaks of Himself as the leader we need as sheep?

If we are defenseless, Jesus is our Defender.

> I am the good shepherd. The good shepherd lays down his life for the sheep (John 10:11).

If we wander aimlessly, Jesus secures us.

> I am the good shepherd. I know my own and my own know me (John 10:14).

If we have no sense of direction, Jesus leads us.

> My sheep hear my voice, and I know them, and they follow me. I give them eternal life, and they will never perish, and no one will snatch them out of my hand (John 10:27-28).

Jesus didn't choose to describe Himself this way arbitrarily. His listeners understood sheep, and many of them were shepherds. They knew what it meant for shepherds to guard their flock from predators. They had no doubt rescued a sheep that

EVEN THOUGH I WALK THROUGH THE VALLEY OF
THE SHADOW OF DEATH, I WILL FEAR NO EVIL, FOR
YOU ARE WITH ME; YOUR ROD AND YOUR STAFF,
THEY COMFORT ME. PSALM 23:4

had wandered from the fold into dangerous territory. They understood the cost to a shepherd of laying down his life for his sheep—of physically and sacrificially attending to their needs and safety. They knew how much direction sheep needed and how easy it was for them to unknowingly find themselves influenced by mob-mentality if they were not shepherded.

Jesus calls Himself the Good Shepherd. He is uniquely qualified to be the lead, to guard, to lay down His life for His sheep. He knows His flock; they are not strangers to Him. He is compassionate, tender, and patient with us, His sheep. Sheep that need our Shepherd's protection, guidance, safekeeping, and direction. Because He is trustworthy, His sheep can rest secure in following Him.

> All the way my Savior leads me;
> What have I to ask beside?
> Can I doubt His tender mercy,
> Who through life has been my guide?

Are you letting Jesus be your guide? Or have you allowed less-worthy ideas, individuals, and things to lead your thoughts and actions? Can you look back on your life and recognize His faithful hand tenderly directing you along the way?

> All the way my Savior leads me;
> Cheers each winding path I tread,
> Gives me grace for ev'ry trial,
> Feeds me with the living bread.

Are you wandering, seeking to satisfy yourself? To feed your own soul? To find fulfillment in your journey when your Shepherd seeks to nourish you, sustain you, provide for your every need?

As these lines from a familiar hymn help us recall to mind: Our Shepherd has never and will never leave us. "I am with you always, to the end of the age" (Matthew 28:20). As our shepherd, Jesus watches over us all through life's journey—even in "the valley of the shadow of death" (Psalm 23:4).

All the way my Savior leads me;
Oh, the fullness of His love!
Perfect rest to me is promised
In my Father's house above.
When my spirit, clothed immortal,
Wings its flight to realms of day,
This my song through endless ages:
Jesus led me all the way;
This my song through endless ages:
Jesus led me all the way.

We need not fear life's winding path, the trials that may come in the darkest valleys, or the unknowns yet to be faced on the journey ahead. Like a shepherd who will not leave any of his flock but will carry those too weak to continue on their own, our Good Shepherd doesn't just lead us out of danger—He carries us to His Father's eternally lush pastures. He leads us all the way home.

GUIDEPOST:

JESUS WATCHES OVER US ALL THROUGH LIFE'S JOURNEY.

WHEN MY SPIRIT, CLOTHED IMMORTAL,
WINGS ITS FLIGHT TO REALMS OF DAY,
THIS MY SONG THROUGH ENDLESS AGES:
JESUS LED ME ALL THE WAY.

take my
life and
let it be
consecrated,
Lord, to Thee.

13

THE DIFFERENCE A SURRENDERED HEART MAKES

An afternoon getting lost in an antique shop is time well spent, in my opinion. I love perusing the stacks of dusty books, some with inscriptions on the front page that stir the imagination: *Who was this "Beloved Harry" to "Your Amelia" in 1912?* I'll wander around, looking for unexpected treasures, curiosities, and discarded gems that must come home to my twenty-first century life.

One time, I came upon a large, albeit dented, brass pitcher. It was substantial and well-crafted, and seemed to have lived a life of nobility somewhere in its previous home and along the journey that led it to the bottom shelf of an antique shop. I picked it up and examined it. It appeared to be intact, capable of holding water, and with a little imagination, I could picture this pitcher holding a most luscious bushel of farmstand flowers. I could imagine it the way it was intended to be: a cleaned and polished vessel of good things.

The only problem, as I contemplated the purchase, was that it looked nothing like that shiny brass pitcher I was imagining. It was tarnished, dirty, a tad rusty in certain spots, and lacking any of its original luster. It looked like an oversized, dingy pot, but because I knew it was brass, I knew what it would take to restore it.

So the pitcher came home with me.

I'm sure you can imagine what followed: I got to work scrubbing it clean with warm, soapy water. Then I applied a brass cleaner and polish, and with some water and a dry cleaning cloth, the pitcher's original luster began emerging. I repeated the process twice more, and with care and the right agent of change, the vessel was restored to its intended state and purpose.

While no illustration or analogy fully captures the wonder of God's work of transformation in a believer's life, my brass pitcher helps me to grasp the work of sanctification in a powerful way.

Don't be put off by the word *sanctification* if it's new to you. *Sanctification* is just a formal way of describing the progressive, ongoing work by which God molds a Christ-follower into His likeness as we trust Him to do the work. We hear the apostle Paul speak of it in...

> Romans 8:29: "Those whom he foreknew he also predestined to be conformed to the image of his Son."

> 2 Corinthians 3:18: "We all, with unveiled face, beholding the glory of the Lord, are being transformed into the same image from one degree of glory to another."

EVERYTHING WE SAY
OR DO WILL EITHER
ILLUMINATE OR OBSCURE
THE CHARACTER OF GOD.
SANCTIFICATION IS THE
PROCESS OF JOYFULLY
GROWING LUMINOUS.

JEN WILKIN

SANCTIFICATION

This process begins at salvation and refers to our growing more and more like Christ as we continue the Christian journey. As we behold our Lord, we become more like Him. And in the end, God's work in us will be made complete, and we will be glorified.

And in...

> Ephesians 5:25-26: "Christ loved the church and gave himself up for her, that he might sanctify her, having cleansed her by the washing of water with the word."

In the same way that my beloved brass pitcher was in a helpless state of ruin and—let's face it—inability to restore itself, we also cannot restore ourselves to our intended state as image-bearers of a holy God. I've heard it said that sanctification is God working in us to transform us into the image-bearers we were meant to be. Sin marred that capacity, and by God's grace through Christ, we are conformed to His likeness little by little, day by day. Jerry Bridges put it this way, reminding us that the transformation isn't merely superficial, but changes us deep within:

> Sanctification is the work of the Holy Spirit in us whereby our inner being is progressively changed, freeing us more and more from sinful traits and developing within us over time the virtues of Christlike character.[8]

What that means for us, believer, is that we don't need to grow impatient with our progress, but we do need to desire progress. We don't control the fruit or the speed at which we arrive at fruitfulness, but we're called to surrender to and abide with the one who promises to change us from the inside out.

Maybe it means that you and I must learn to align our hearts with the truths in these familiar hymn lyrics:

Take my life and let it be
consecrated, Lord, to thee.

Take my moments and my days;
let them flow in endless praise,
let them flow in endless praise.

Take my hands and let them move
at the impulse of thy love.
Take my feet and let them be
swift and beautiful for thee,
swift and beautiful for thee.

Take my voice and let me sing
always, only, for my King.
Take my lips and let them be
filled with messages from thee,
filled with messages from thee.

Take my silver and my gold;
not a mite would I withhold.
Take my intellect and use
every power as thou shalt choose,
every power as thou shalt choose.

Take my will and make it thine;
it shall be no longer mine.
Take my heart it is thine own;
it shall be thy royal throne,
it shall be thy royal throne.

Take my love; my Lord, I pour
at thy feet its treasure store.
Take myself, and I will be
ever, only, all for thee,
ever, only, all for thee.

The hymn writer leaves no stone unturned here. She truly surrenders and invites the Lord to bring everything in her life into alignment with God's

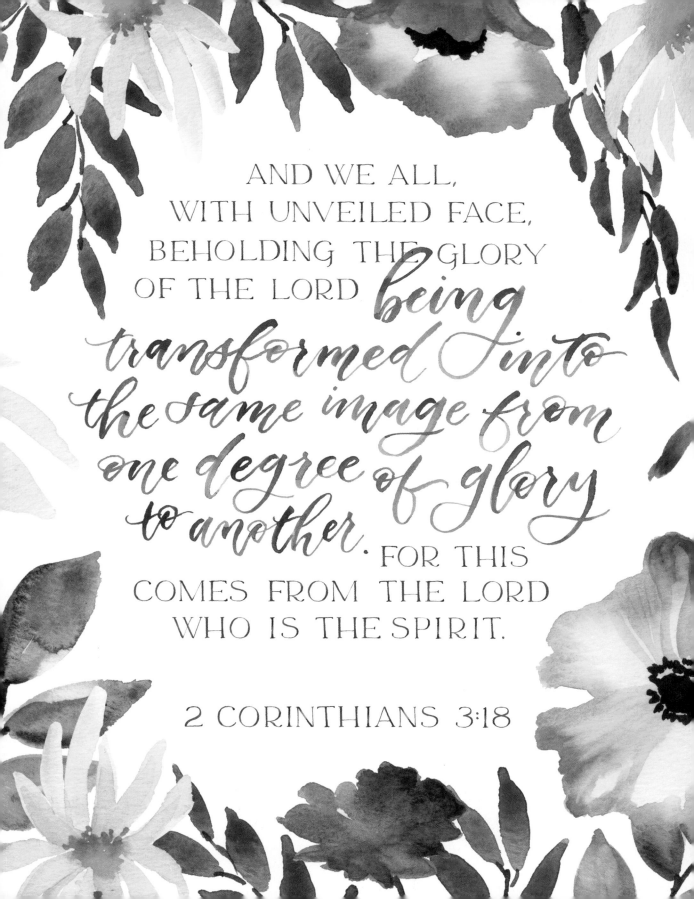

AND WE ALL,
WITH UNVEILED FACE,
BEHOLDING THE GLORY
OF THE LORD *being*
transformed into
the same image from
one degree of glory
to another. FOR THIS
COMES FROM THE LORD
WHO IS THE SPIRIT.

2 CORINTHIANS 3:18

will. She wants Him to make her more like Him. She wants to be sanctified for His good purposes and glory. Ever, only, all for Thee, God.

So when on life's journey we begin to doubt our progress as a child of God...when we fear we've somehow missed His transformational power in our lives, remember that Christ is the sanctifier—it is *His* job. "He who began a good work in you will bring it to completion at the day of Jesus Christ" (Philippians 1:6). Remember? The Lord will complete the work He has begun in you. You need only be faithful to yield to Him and abide in Him as He does His good work in you.

GUIDEPOST:

THE LORD WILL COMPLETE THE WORK HE HAS BEGUN IN US.

He will hold me fast,
He will hold me fast;
For my Savior loves me so,
He will hold me fast.

14

SECURE IN HIS ALMIGHTY HAND

Several years ago, our family walked through a season of loss. We'd invested deeply in a community and an endeavor that we could no longer continue in. It wasn't cancer, but there was no cure to what was ailing us. It wasn't divorce, but the parting was painful. It wasn't death, but we said our goodbyes. Our family's journey with God had seen mountains and valleys, but nothing had stung like this particular season of sadness, confusion, and a sudden detour in the road we were so sure God had placed us on.

Whirling. Swirling. Chaos. Questions. Fear. Bitterness. Fumbling. Shame. Strain. Why? How? What if...?

I remember knowing with my mind that God had a plan, but feeling like the sky was falling. That summer, we took a few days to retreat to the mountains of Colorado. A dear friend joined us, and she and I journeyed back home together. While driving the long desert interstate that crossed Colorado into New Mexico, storms began to build across the horizon. The summer monsoon season can be epic in the Southwest. From our vantage, I could see multiple storms building and encircling us. To the east, lightning shook and thunder clapped. To the west, sheets of rain fell from yet another storm cell and created a delicate veil that, from a distance, looked soft but was no doubt torrential at its core. And as we headed south, we could see that we were journeying toward an ominous, violent build-up of clouds—the darkest, most foreboding storm of all of them, looming over the mountains ahead.

And yet, just behind us, to the north, the sun peeked through the clouds, revealing blue skies. A faint rainbow began to form, and I caught a glimpse of it in the rear-view mirror.

As I scanned that entire 360-degree radius, I could see storms both raging on and being stilled. I looked over to my friend, and with tears in my eyes, blurted, "If He can hold the sky together, He can hold us."

The mercy of driving through an all-encompassing storm, both figuratively and literally, was seeing the sovereignty of God on display. It was as if He was saying, "I am in control. You can't calm the storm, but I can. You can't hold all things together; that's My job."

In fact, it is:

> By him all things were created, in heaven and on earth, visible and invisible, whether thrones or dominions or rulers or authorities—all things were created through him and for him. And he is before all things, and in him all things hold together (Colossians 1:16-17).

Paul, who penned this description of Christ in Colossians, knew something about the power of torrential storms as one who'd been shipwrecked. He knew something about the power of rulers and authorities as one who'd been imprisoned for his faith. He knew something about trials, suffering, and impossible

God's plan will continue on God's schedule.

A.W. TOZER

THE SOVEREIGNTY OF GOD

God's rule over all creation is absolute. Nothing can overrule Him or happen outside of His plans. While His authority is unlimited, everything He does is done in a manner that is consistent with His good and perfect character. Because of God's sovereignty, we can rest knowing that every circumstance in our lives is in His more-than-capable hands.

circumstances. He had experienced betrayal, loss of friendship, the parting of ways in ministry, and the ache of journeying alone. And yet Paul knew the sovereignty of God and His power. He believed and served a God who holds all things together. As Joni Eareckson Tada says,

> Nothing is a surprise to God; nothing is a setback to His plans; nothing can thwart His purposes; and nothing is beyond His control. His sovereignty is absolute. Everything that happens is uniquely ordained by God. Sovereignty is a weighty thing to ascribe to the nature and character of God. Yet if He were not sovereign, He would not be God. The Bible is clear that God is in control of everything that happens.[9]

By God's mighty hand, we are secure. By His Word, all creation was made. By His love, His children are brought near. By His will, His purposes and plans are fulfilled in our lives.

Of all the ways Paul could describe how God is sovereign, he chose to use the word "hold" (Colossians 1:17). Though he would have been justified to do so, Paul didn't say that "in Him, all things are ruled." Paul wanted to make it clear to his readers that Christ's authority, pre-eminence, and omnipotence were not expressions of a power trip, but were manifest out of His great love for His creation. Holding hardly happens at arm's length; holding happens when strong arms want to keep precious cargo nearby. We hold what we don't want to lose; we hold what we call our own.

I'm reminded of these comforting truths penned in 1906:

When I fear my faith will fail,
Christ will hold me fast;
When the tempter would prevail,
He will hold me fast.
He will hold me fast,
He will hold me fast;
For my Savior loves me so,
He will hold me fast.

My guess is you've known such a season too. Maybe you're in that season now. Perhaps your journey is taking you straight into the worst of a storm, and there's nothing you can do to fix it, thwart it, calm it, or control it. God is our good Father, friend. In the same way a good parent invites a child onto his or her lap and holds the child in assurance, we can put our trust in the one who doesn't just hold creation together, but our lives as well.

God's sovereignty exists in harmony with His other attributes. In Christ, there is no path or journey assigned through His sovereignty that doesn't lead you to His provision. Spurgeon said it well: "The wheel of providence revolves, but its axle is eternal love."[10]

So look up, pilgrim. Look all around you. Is God at work as the wheel of providence turns? Did He cause the sun to rise without your help? He is, and He did. If He can hold the seasons and the skies together by His love and omnipotence, He can hold you and me. The God who holds the universe in His hands holds us in His hands.

GUIDEPOST:

THE GOD WHO HOLDS THE UNIVERSE IN HIS HANDS HOLDS US IN HIS HANDS.

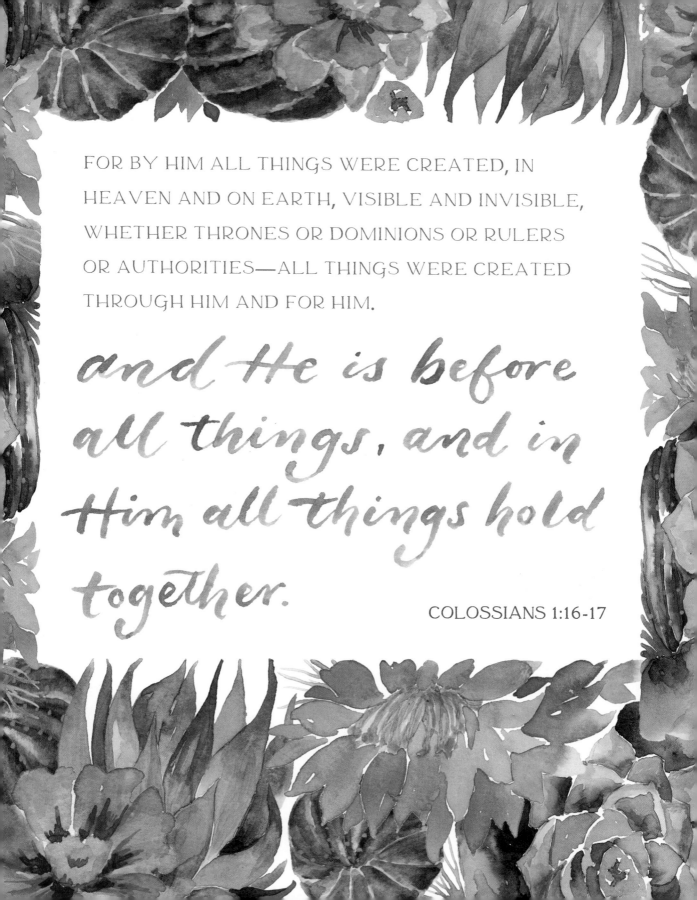

FOR BY HIM ALL THINGS WERE CREATED, IN HEAVEN AND ON EARTH, VISIBLE AND INVISIBLE, WHETHER THRONES OR DOMINIONS OR RULERS OR AUTHORITIES—ALL THINGS WERE CREATED THROUGH HIM AND FOR HIM.

and He is before all things, and in Him all things hold together.

COLOSSIANS 1:16-17

15

GREATER THAN ANY DIFFICULTY

The Colorado Trail, a popular trek in our area of Colorado, runs between Denver and Durango. It's 486 miles in length, averages 10,300 feet above sea level, and reaches 13,271 feet elevation at its highest point. If you're an outdoor enthusiast, this might sound like a perfect way to spend a few weeks of your life; for me, it sounds like a good way to fall off a cliff to my demise.

If you're going to backpack this rigorous trail, it'll take two or three weeks to cover on mountain bikes and weeks longer on foot. I marvel at the amount of planning it takes to have enough sustenance along the way. How do you make sure you have enough water for such a journey? For all the nonhikers among us: the answer is a water filtration system. And what about food? I hear dehydrated meal packs are tasty when you're super hungry. And that's just if things go smoothly and as planned. Throw in gear malfunctions, accidental losses, or torrential storms, and even the best provisions may not sustain you.

It's never the start of any journey that concerns us. It's during the long stretch in the middle that we grow weary and worry about water, food, and stamina. No matter how much you pack or prepare, a long journey

GOD AS SUSTAINER

God's care for us is unceasing. At all times, He knows exactly what we need, and His provision will always be sufficient. For this reason, we can cast all our cares upon Him, and we can say, "Surely goodness and mercy shall follow me all the days of my life" (Psalm 23:6).

will always require replenishment of supplies along the way. Very simply, we are not self-sustaining.

For many of us, the fact we're not self-sustaining seems hard to swallow if you look at the way we live our lives. We don't welcome weakness. We are determined to do whatever it takes to make it to the finish line. The world is constantly telling us to be self-reliant and to take control of our lives through self-betterment. All this cultivates a mindset of believing we can sustain ourselves through strategic living and good choices.

But so often, as we journey, we encounter conditions and circumstances that pay no regard to how carefully we planned ahead. The unexpected loss of a job, financial strain, capsizing conflicts in relationships. We work to avoid derailing difficulties, and we attempt to always stay one step ahead of unwanted circumstances. Sometimes we wear ourselves out trying to be self-sustaining. I can think of specific seasons when my family and I have known these and other trials—obstacles we wouldn't have chosen to write into our pilgrim stories. My guess is that you've encountered similar challenges and may very well be navigating them even now. I imagine that, like me, you've grown weary of trying to hold it all together, as if everything you need to keep on keeping on has to come from you.

Perhaps you've tried to outrun lack and limitation with your own resources. Take heart, friend. God desires for you to rediscover, or realize for the first time, that He alone is your sustainer.

My grace is sufficient for you, for my power is made perfect in weakness.

2 CORINTHIANS 12:9

The apostle Paul knew Him as such and wrote of the Lord's response amidst his need for provision and relief: "He said to me, 'My grace is sufficient for you, for my power is made perfect in weakness.' Therefore I will boast all the more gladly of my weaknesses, so that the power of Christ may rest upon me" (2 Corinthians 12:9).

Everything God says here is counterintuitive to our innate self-reliance. The focus here isn't our weakness; it's God's sustenance. The gloriousness of God's declaration here is that we can never outrun His ability to sustain us; He *desires* to be our sufficiency. And Paul's discovery that he passes on to his reader? It's this: When we know and trust the character of God, we become more willing to let Him work through our weaknesses and display His strength and power.

It makes no sense to try to outrun our lack when our very inability to sustain ourselves is God's great opportunity to provide. Despite what we want to feel or believe, we never stop existing in weakness as fallen and finite beings. *We are ever-weak, and God is ever-sustaining.*

God never stops sustaining—strengthening, carrying, providing, guarding, upholding, supporting, protecting, leading, sheltering, rescuing, comforting, preserving. He never stops sustaining because He's created us to never not need Him. God is not a sustainer like a genie in a bottle, who is called on for limited wishes. God is always and perpetually the sustainer of our lives.

Do you feel physically weak and weary?

God promises to keep you and carry you for the days He has for you. "Even to your old age and gray hairs I am he, I am he who will sustain you. I have made you and I will carry you; I will sustain you and I will rescue you" (Isaiah 46:4 NIV).

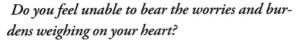

Do you feel unable to bear the worries and burdens weighing on your heart?

God is strong enough to bear them for you. "Cast your burden on the LORD, and he will sustain you; he will never permit the righteous to be moved" (Psalm 55:22).

Do you lack courage to continue your journey?

God will give you perseverance. "My flesh and my heart may fail, but God is the strength of my heart and my portion forever" (Psalm 73:26).

Do you struggle with motivation or purpose?

God sustains us by His will. "In him we live and move and have our being" (Acts 17:28).

You see, our Sustainer, God, accompanies us on our journey and continually supplies us with all that we need *as we go*. He's not a mere midway stop. He's not a refueling station. He's not a mediocre alternative to our own supplies. He *is* our sustenance by being, Himself, the provision we need most. And like the psalmist who preaches to his own heart, the hymn writer of these comforting lyrics calls us to remind our souls to rest and trust our sustaining God. I'm borrowing these words:

> *Be still, my soul! the Lord is on thy side;*
> *Bear patiently the cross of grief or pain.*
> *Leave to your God to order and provide;*
> *In every change He faithful will remain.*
> *Be still, my soul! your best, your heav'nly Friend*
> *Thro' thorny ways leads to a joyful end.*
>
> *Be still, my soul! your God doth undertake*
> *To guide the future as He has the past.*
> *Your hope, your confidence let nothing shake;*
> *All now mysterious shall be bright at last.*
> *Be still, my soul! the waves and winds still know*
> *His voice who ruled them while He dwelt below.*

HE GIVETH MORE GRACE
WHEN THE BURDENS GROW GREATER,

HE SENDETH MORE STRENGTH
WHEN THE LABOURS INCREASE;

TO ADDED AFFLICTION
HE ADDETH HIS MERCY,

TO MULTIPLIED TRIALS,
HIS MULTIPLIED PEACE.

ANNIE JOHNSON FLINT

In every change He faithful will remain. Our pilgrim journeys will take more stamina than we possess, more provisions than we can gather, and more perseverance than we can muster. Our paths will reach heights and lows that rival any trail through any mountain range. Continuing onward will feel impossible at times. But friend, don't be surprised if your travels require more than the resources you have. Our good Father lovingly designed it that way. He delights in being your Sustainer—the provider of strength in your weakness. And no matter how great the difficulty you face, God is greater.

GUIDEPOST:

NO MATTER HOW GREAT THE DIFFICULTY WE FACE, GOD IS GREATER.

16

NEVER A REASON TO WORRY

The older I get, the more I'm convinced that to truly trust is almost rarer than love. We can say the words "I love you" to a friend or our spouse, but we struggle to live the words "I trust you" due to our pride and self-sufficiency. Maybe you've found this to be true in your life as well: It's easier to profess feelings of adoration than it is to be unguarded in a relationship. It's easy to enjoy companionship, but hard to not worry that that same companion will never leave us, betray us, or go back on his or her word.

Some of us have known the sting of choosing to be vulnerable only to experience a break of trust. Some of us have grown thick-skinned along the way and enter relationships with one eye on the exit and our hands clenched to the steering wheel. "I won't be hurt again," we murmur behind our socially acceptable smiles. "The only person you can really count on is yourself," we let ourselves believe.

It's exhausting to be so guarded. But let's not sugarcoat this: Trustworthiness can be so rare when we're journeying with other sinful, broken pilgrims.

What a relief it is that God's Word tells honestly of the ways His faithful servants also experienced disappointment, betrayal, and broken promises. Remember Joseph, betrayed by his brothers, left in Pharaoh's dungeon? Think about Jacob's father-in-law, Laban, who tricked Jacob into marrying both his daughters. Then there's Paul, who was abandoned by Demas. In fact, Jesus Himself knew the sting of abandonment from those He shared His life with most. He was no stranger to the lack of trustworthiness in our broken world, and neither were the people whom God loved and included in the story of redemption.

Encountering betrayal from others on our journeys won't threaten to derail us if we grasp that God is the *only* one who is truly trustworthy. When we know the character of God, we won't rely on feelings, empty promises, or trust on blind faith. We will go to the Word of God. We will consider who He always was and who He always will be; we will *know* Him.

> Those who know your name put their trust in you, for you, O LORD, have not forsaken those who seek you (Psalm 9:10).

You see, we were meant to live in the confidence of knowing the trustworthiness of God. All through life, other companions may abandon us, disappoint us, or lead us down the wrong path, but not with the Lord. He is the most trustworthy guide we could have as pilgrims on a long journey. He cannot lie, He can only do good, and He is bound by the lovingkindness that defines Him. All His attributes work in unison; we do not trust a God who contradicts Himself, but a God who proves His trustworthiness again and again through all His ways and all His works.

He lights the path before us (Psalm 119:105).
He guides and leads (Proverbs 3:5-6).
He sees and vindicates (Psalm 37:5-6).
He will never abandon us (Hebrews 13:5).
He will keep every promise He has made to us (1 Kings 8:56).
He will strengthen and protect us from the evil one (2 Thessalonians 3:3).
He will answer us in our distress (Psalm 20:1).

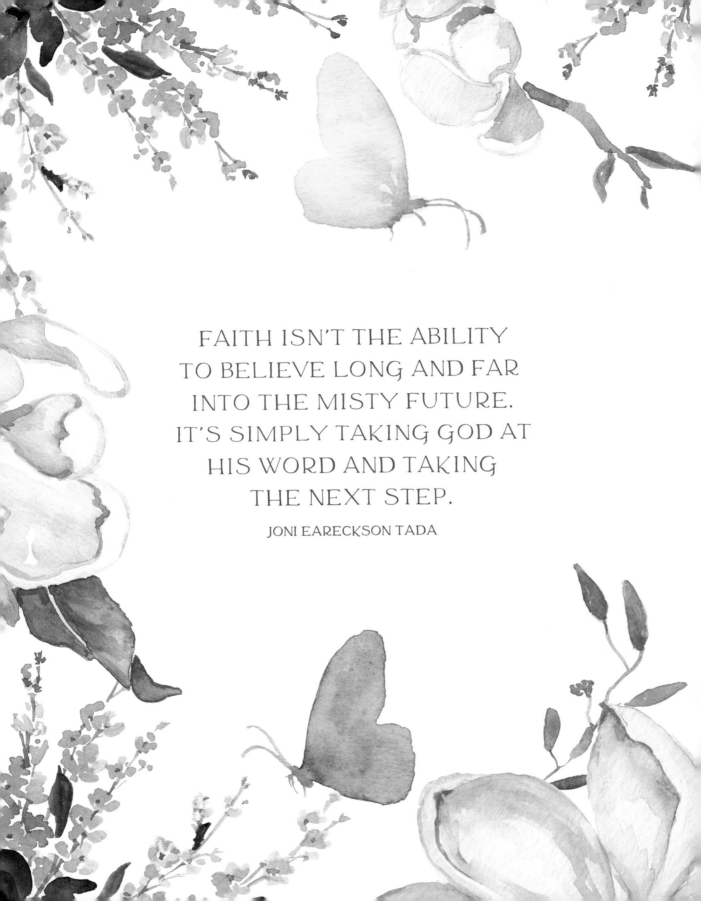

FAITH ISN'T THE ABILITY
TO BELIEVE LONG AND FAR
INTO THE MISTY FUTURE.
IT'S SIMPLY TAKING GOD AT
HIS WORD AND TAKING
THE NEXT STEP.

JONI EARECKSON TADA

THE TRUSTWORTHINESS OF GOD

God has never failed to keep any of His promises. What He says He will do, He does. Even in times when we wonder if He has forgotten us, we can have absolute assurance that He will never forsake us. Our feelings may lead us to doubt, but the evidence of God's care for us in the past should assure us of His continued care in the future.

He will continue to do His sanctifying work in us
(Philippians 1:6).
He is our rock, our refuge, our stronghold (2 Samuel 22:3).
He is with us even in the valley of the shadow of death
(Psalm 23:4).

How trustworthy is our God!

Paul David Tripp says it well: "When Christ is my hope, he becomes the one thing in which I have confidence. I act on his wisdom and I bank on his grace. I trust his promises and I rely on his presence. And I pursue all the good things that he has promised me simply because I trust him."[11]

Are you banking on God's grace? Is He your hope? Recount the ways He has been faithful as He's promised here. Stop to consider how trustworthy He's been in times past, perhaps when you've not even realized or thanked Him for it. This very trustworthiness you have experienced in the past can be counted on in the future. If you and I would take the time to write out the ways God's been trustworthy in our lives, we, too, will echo this refrain:

'Tis so sweet, to trust in Jesus,
Just to take Him at His word;
Just to rest upon His promise;
Just to know, Thus says the Lord.

Jesus, Jesus, how I trust Him
  How I've proved Him o'er and o'er,
Jesus, Jesus, precious Jesus!
O for grace to trust Him more.

Faithful Father, You alone are truly trustworthy; give us the grace to trust you more.

— GUIDEPOST: —

BECAUSE GOD HAS PROVEN HIMSELF TRUSTWORTHY IN THE PAST, WE CAN TRUST HIM WITH OUR FUTURE.

Those who know your name put their trust in you, for you, O Lord, have not forsaken those who seek you.

Psalm 9:10

Thou changest not, Thy compassions they fail not; As Thou hast been, Thou forever wilt be.

17

EVER, ALWAYS, ETERNALLY TRUE

Before the stars formed constellations in the sky...
Before the waters carved streams out of the wilderness...
Before every wonderful thing we've ever known...
God's faithfulness already and always was.

He's been faithful forever, long before you even believed that He was. Hebrews 13:8 comforts with clarity: "Jesus Christ is the same yesterday and today and forever."

I don't know about you, but right now—in the midst of so much that is upside-down in our world—*unchanging faithfulness* seems too good to be true. Fashion trends, social-media platform algorithms, popular opinions, diet and exercise musts. They're ever-changing. (Do you remember when margarine was preferred over butter? When breakfast was non-negotiable? When grains and carbohydrates took up the largest portion of the nutritional pyramid?) Regardless of your age, you've likely experienced significant change in your lifetime. By nature, human beings are capricious creatures, rarely

THE FAITHFULNESS OF GOD

The evidence of God's faithfulness is made clear to us all through the Scriptures. The God who was faithful to our favorite men and women of the Bible is the same God who is faithful to us today. The fact that He is faithful means we can safely place our full trust in Him. And this, in turn, should provide us with an incredible sense of security.

content, eager for change, and constantly looking for more or better. It's a constant struggle in my own life.

But this is not God's nature. He is trustworthy, reliable, unshakable, and incapable of going back on His Word. His faithfulness has never and will never change; our God is *immutable*.

Think back as far as you can. Where does your story begin? Do you think of a place? A person? A feeling? I'm thinking of my story as beginning in the city of Taipei, Taiwan. In a little apartment filled with love and my mother's nursery rhymes in Mandarin. Maybe you, like me, have been conditioned to believe that your life's journey is a sum of wins and failures, delights and sorrows, what you've done and all that you've failed to do. And perhaps you, too, have been told that you control your own story, and you've been tempted to believe it. It's not hard to buy into such a narrative in this manifesting, dream-chasing, self-perfecting age of opportunity we live in.

The psalmist didn't have shelves of self-help books to contend with, but he no doubt knew the limitations of a life-strategy dependent on his own strength and achievement...the fallenness of self-reliance. He knew the desperation of coming to the end of himself and his own strength and looking to his Creator, God. I imagine the psalmist—weary and afflicted—out in the barren desert. With

MY SECURITY AS A CHRISTIAN
DOES NOT RESIDE IN THE
STRENGTH OF MY FAITH BUT
IN THE INDESTRUCTIBILITY
OF MY SAVIOR.

SINCLAIR FERGUSON

humility and deep need, he sighs and looks up into the night sky. Overwhelmed by the majesty and infiniteness of God's creation, he reminds his soul and acknowledges with his lips the faithful, unchanging, eternality of God. Is it any wonder he would declare to the Lord: "The heavens are the work of your hands. They will perish, but you will remain"? (Psalm 102:25-26).

When we are faithless, God remains faithful (2 Timothy 2:13).

When we are fickle, God remains unchanging (Hebrews 13:8).

When we fail, God remains a promise keeper (Romans 4:21).

The hero of your story is the faithfulness of God. We may feel unsure about our ever-changing life circumstances, but our God is fully and eternally trustworthy in His unchanging faithfulness toward us, His children.

Because we can say of our God...

There is no shadow of turning with Thee.
Thou changest not, Thy compassions, they fail not;
As Thou hast been, Thou forever wilt be.

...we need not fear. We can trust in a God who was faithful before our stories began.

I can't help but wonder as I think of all the ways God makes His unchanging faithfulness known to us: Could it be that my fear and desire to control the outcomes in my life have more to do with my thinking less-than-adequate thoughts about God than my seemingly worrisome circumstances? How would I view my story differently if my security was wrapped up in the immutability of God? What if I followed Jeremiah's lead, as expressed by him in these words from Lamentations 3:19-23?

I remember my affliction and my wandering,
    the bitterness and the gall.
I well remember them,
    and my soul is downcast within me.

Yet this I call to mind
    and therefore I have hope:

Because of the LORD's great love we are not consumed,
    for his compassions never fail.
They are new every morning;
    great is your faithfulness.

An indestructible Savior. An unchanging King. An eternal Father. Our immutable God. You see, change is frightening for the ones who rely only on themselves. But when our security and confidence is in our great and faithful God, no twists or turns have the power to derail us.

This pilgrim journey you're on, friend? It will be shaped most fully by whether your hope lies in doing more, being better, and never failing along the way...

...or if you choose to set your hope in this:

As thou hast been, thou forever wilt be.

Great is Thy faithfulness, Lord. Let me follow where Your unchanging, eternal, unconditional reliability leads. You are faithful and will never fail us.

GUIDEPOST:

GOD IS FAITHFUL AND WILL NEVER FAIL US.

Jesus Christ is the same yesterday and today and forever.

HEBREWS 13:8

Come, thou Fount of every blessing, tune my heart to sing thy grace;

STREAMS OF MERCY, NEVER CEASING, CALL FOR SONGS OF LOUDEST PRAISE.

18

GRATITUDE IN EVERY CIRCUMSTANCE

Where I live in the mountains of southwest Colorado, rain is coveted, especially in the summertime when wildfires threaten the arid terrain. Typically, during monsoon season in July, the clouds start rolling in during the afternoon, and dark clouds form over the peaks and valleys around my home. They build and build, and when they can no longer hold one more drop of moisture, the heavens break loose, and the downpour we hope for comes crashing down. There's nothing like a good summer rainstorm. I'm convinced everything grows better (including me) when dry ground has experienced a proper soaking.

The earth feels and smells different after the rain. It's as if the rain magnifies every leaf texture, the minerals in the soil, and heightens our very senses. I don't know about you, but I always become very aware of what was dull before the rain.

I think of the line from one of my most beloved hymns, "Come, Thou Fount of Every Blessing," and how there's something about God's mercies that washes away our dimmed perceptions and stirs a greater awareness of His kind and good gifts:

Come, thou Fount of every blessing,
tune my heart to sing thy grace;
streams of mercy, never ceasing,
call for songs of loudest praise.

Teach me some melodious sonnet,
sung by flaming tongues above.
Praise the mount I'm fixed upon it
mount of God's redeeming love.

Much like the rains that bring clarity and augment the earth's characteristics after the storm, the deluge of God's good gifts—recounted in God's Word and through the testimonies of our lives—helps us to see with greater awareness His kindness in our lives. The vibrancy of His faithfulness is so often dulled when our perceptions are clouded by the dust storms of false narratives and self-centered thoughts that drive our hearts far from praise.

I don't know about you, but my heart feels out of tune most days. When I'm not in tune, it feels as if competing melodies are vying for my attention and affections as I seek to lift up praises to God. When I'm out of tune, usually it's because I'm distracted by thoughts that do not align with the Word of God. Misalignment leads to misperception, causing us to believe discordant thoughts:

I can't do this.
This feels impossible.
Will I ever change?
All I need is to get better at...
I don't have any real friends.
Is everyone disappointed with me?
Why am I such a mess?

Thanksgiving
IS GOOD BUT
thanks-living
IS BETTER.

MATTHEW HENRY

THE PRAISEWORTHINESS OF GOD

The prophet Isaiah wrote, "O LORD, you are my God; I will exalt you; I will praise your name, for you have done wonderful things" (Isaiah 25:1). When we recognize and profess God's goodness, our hearts cannot help but be lifted up in praise. In fact, it is against the backdrop of life's disappointments that God's goodness stands out to us all the more. He is worthy!

You and I know these and so many other discordant thoughts do not line up with what is true about who we are in Christ. And yet we allow the dissonant melodies to play as the soundtracks to our daily lives...and accompany us on our journey with Christ. How do we replace these thoughts with the melody of God's goodness?

An athlete training for a marathon (or any race) often chooses a playlist to train to—a list that motivates, energizes, and helps the person to stay the course. I'm no athlete, but I don't think I'd choose to listen to melancholy, slow-paced music if I were hoping to run the race with speed and agility. But so many of us are running our race—our Christian lives—with the wrong playlist, and we wonder why we don't run with courage, confidence, and power.

Gratitude is the soundtrack we're meant to run our race to.

Paul tells us in 1 Thessalonians 5:18, "Give thanks in all circumstances; for this is the will of God in Christ Jesus for you." Giving thanks isn't to be limited to the highlight-reel moments of our lives; we're to express our gratefulness even in the mundane, ordinary times. Gratitude is God's plan for us—for our good and for the peace that we so long to have. We will not experience the peace that surpasses all understanding until we surrender our burdens to God and give thanks to Him (Philippians 4:6-7).

You see, giving thanks isn't a magic pill that fixes everything; it helps our hearts be retuned (and returned) to what is true and worthy. Do you feel as though you're viewing your circumstances through the fog of frustration and faithlessness? Does the soundtrack you're playing as you continue your journey sing words of truth or discordant lies?

Why does the fount of God's blessings—the realities of His mercy and grace—call for songs of loudest praise, as the hymn suggests?

I think it has something to do with what the psalmist does again and again when he recalls the faithful works of God and the abundance of His blessings. Psalm 107 begins with "Oh give thanks to the LORD, for he is good, for his steadfast love endures forever!" And after the psalmist recounts and declares God's power, goodness, and faithfulness, he sums everything up by penning, "Whoever is wise, let him attend to these things; let them consider the steadfast love of the LORD" (verse 43).

There's wisdom in "attending to these things"—to a true consideration of God's love. In the same way that a song gets stuck in our head, a soundtrack filled with the truth of God's faithfulness will dislodge any self-centered discontent within us. Can a heart overflowing with gratitude for what God has given us keep us from speaking and living a praise-filled life?

I can't help but see the thread that connects it all:

Recount the love of God

→ a heart retuned

→ alignment with true treasure

→ ability to rejoice and access to peace

→ overflowing with gratitude and praise

→ wisdom to keep running the race

Grateful praise isn't merely a good idea; it's imperative.

Oh give thanks
to the Lord,
for he is good,
for his steadfast
love endures
forever!

PSALM 107:1

The fount of God's grace is immeasurable and will never run out. That's good news for us, friend, because it means that our gratitude also has no end. If we were made for praise, if we are to give thanks in all things, and if we are to know peace by giving thanks, we can trust that God Himself will provide for the retuning of heart we're meant to know. Matthew Henry said it best: "Thanksgiving is good but thanks-living is better."[12]

There's nothing like a retuned heart that sings His praise. Praising God in every situation enables us to have gratitude in every situation.

GUIDEPOST:

PRAISING GOD IN EVERY SITUATION ENABLES US TO HAVE GRATITUDE IN EVERY SITUATION.

a mighty
fortress is our
God, a bulwark
never failing.

DID WE IN OUR OWN STRENGTH CONFIDE,

OUR STRIVING WOULD BE LOSING.

19

A SHIELD THAT PROTECTS

Some of the best travel tales involve peril and danger; they're just not the journeys we'd ever sign up for. We're entertained by the game of survival in Jumanji, but no one wants to meet wild animals and treacherous terrain around every corner. The ingenuity and bonding that the Swiss Family Robinson experienced is admirable, but I can't think of anyone eager for the opportunity to be shipwrecked on an island with no resources. We admire what's produced in the course of the most trying journeys; we just wish they didn't have to be so difficult.

Lord, can I have a heart that's bent heavenward without the ache of a body bent and broken on this earth?

Lord, can't You let me experience true gratitude without having to lose something valuable first?

Lord, do I have to know what darkness feels like in order to truly appreciate the light?

Lord, is it absolutely necessary for me to know weakness if I want to discover Your power and strength?

Lord, can't You teach me to put my trust in You without having my faith put to the test?

Do these questions sound familiar to you too? I so often want God's deliverance without having to experience the *need* for deliverance. I want to know His mighty hand of protection, but I don't want the fear that drives me to find Him faithful.

GOD AS DELIVERER

The story of God's people always has been and always will be a story of deliverance. God does not call us to fight our battles alone. He invites us to seek refuge in Him, to trust Him to carry us through life's storms. The path to heaven is filled with perils, but nothing can pluck us from God's protective hands, which will lead us safely home.

The heavenward journey is fraught with peril. The path for the Christ-follower is not always lined with daisies, lush moss, and bubbling brooks. Some parts of our journey, yes, but more often than not, we face obstacles that seem unsurpassable, steep climbs that feel impossible, and dark valleys we don't know how to navigate. We face storms that beat us down and threaten to undo us. And not unlike the enemies who lurk in some of our favorite tales of adventure, we, too, face dangers and snares that we fear might take us off course from our destination.

The famous tale *The Pilgrim's Progress* is a story of perseverance. As Christian makes his way from the City of Destruction to the City of God, he encounters other travelers who have quit or turned back. He himself faces dangers and temptations and wonders whether he should give up. He experiences weakness, discouragement, and obstacles. The allegory so aptly depicts our journeys with Christ: The path is more difficult than most anticipate, but God's faithfulness to deliver and sustain is more present than most realize.

The psalmist discovered God's deliverance in the midst of his dangerous journey, and wrote:

> The Lord is my rock and my fortress and my deliverer, my God, my rock, in whom I take refuge, my shield, and the horn of my salvation, my stronghold (Psalm 18:2).

The whole of Psalm 18 is a depiction of God as rescuer. The psalmist doesn't call the Lord his deliverer on account of God causing his troubles to disappear. No, the psalmist describes how he called out to God, who helped him *in the midst* of the most dangerous, treacherous, enemy-filled circumstances. He found God faithful during every part of his journey, including those he would've rather not had to endure.

ONE WITH GOD
IS A MAJORITY.

WILLIAM CAREY

During fearful times...
In the midst of the unwanted circumstances...
While the difficult situation has not yet been resolved...

You see, our God is a deliverer. That's who He is. He delights to show us His faithfulness in the most impossible circumstances. He delivered Joseph from a pit and a prison. He delivered Noah and his family from a flood that destroyed the earth. He delivered Moses as a baby, and again with all the Hebrews when they fled Egypt. He delivered Israel multiple times through the era of the judges, and David from all his enemies. He delivered Daniel from lions and Jonah from a fish. He delivered Jesus' family when Herod wanted to kill the child who had been born a king. In each of these accounts from Scripture, God chose to show His deliverance in and through the most difficult and unwanted circumstances faced by His children. Would they have praised God for His deliverance if not for circumstances that revealed their lack and limitations, and required His help?

Would we cry out for rescue if not for the spiritual, physical, and emotional needs we encounter in our everyday lives—needs that reveal our greatest need for God, our Deliverer?

The evidence of our own lives would suggest otherwise.

A mighty fortress is our God!

We weren't meant to navigate the dangers and difficulties of life's journeys in our own strength—in fact, we can't. We simply don't have the resources to rescue ourselves and to secure our own way:

> *Did we in our own strength confide,*
> *Our striving would be losing,*
> *Were not the right Man on our side,*
> *The Man of God's own choosing.*
> *Dost ask who that may be?*
> *Christ Jesus, it is He;*

Lord Sabaoth His name,
From age to age the same;
And He must win the battle.

Just as the psalmist declared in Psalm 18, God is our deliverer, our shield, our protection, our victor. He never promised us a painless journey (in fact, we are told the opposite), but He promises to be the Deliverer who sees us through the very journey He marks out for us. No enemy can threaten to derail what God has secured, and no lurking danger can snatch you from the shield of God's faithfulness. There is nothing you face in your journey that God hasn't already chosen to show His faithfulness to carry you through.

Our weary and fearful experiences do not surprise Him. In the same way that His plans and purposes as Deliverer were ever-present with Joseph, Moses, David, and Daniel, He is with us as Christ-followers. We already have a Deliverer in the person of Christ, who—as we dwell with Him and He in us—more than rescues us from unwanted circumstances and difficult detours; He delivers us from the futile attempt to survive through striving.

Remember:

> Through many dangers, toils and snares I have already come;
> 'Tis grace hath brought me safe thus far, and grace will lead me home.[13]

God wins the battles we would lose in our own strength.

So, never mind the difficult road ahead and the pitfalls all around. Instead, call on God. Your heaven-bound story is exactly what He has written in order for you to find Him a mighty fortress. He can't wait to answer you with His faithfulness and to shield you by His love. That's just who He is, and always will be. As your Deliverer, nothing can keep God from bringing you safely home.

GUIDEPOST:

AS OUR DELIVERER, NOTHING CAN KEEP GOD FROM BRINGING US SAFELY HOME.

The LORD is my rock and my fortress and my deliverer, my God, my rock, in whom I take refuge, my shield, and the horn of my salvation, my stronghold.

Psalm 18:2

HOLY, HOLY,
HOLY! THOUGH THE
DARKNESS HIDE THEE,
THOUGH THE EYE OF
SINFUL MAN THY GLORY MAY NOT
SEE; ONLY THOU ART HOLY;
THERE IS NONE BESIDE THEE,
PERFECT IN POWER, LOVE
AND PURITY.

20

GROWING INTO HIS LIKENESS

In an effort to make God relatable and accessible to those who don't know Him, Christians are often tempted to downplay God's holiness and make Him out to be a pal who was no more than "one of us," as one secular song suggested in the 1990s. They may even describe God as benevolent without any mention of His justice, and merciful sans any obligation to His wholly sinless, transcendent nature. But to speak of Him without acknowledging His holiness is to not really speak of Him at all.

Holiness is the single most significant attribute of God because it is from God's holiness that every other foundational truth exists. Sam Storms says it this way: "The holiness of God only secondarily refers to His moral purity, His righteousness of character. It primarily points to His *infinite otherness*. To say that God is holy is to say that He is *transcendentally separate*. Holiness is not one attribute among many. It is not like grace or power or knowledge or wrath. Everything about God is holy. Each attribute partakes of divine holiness."[14]

Moses and the people of Israel sang praise, and asked rhetorically, in Exodus 15:11, "Who is like you, O LORD, among the gods? Who is like you, majestic in holiness, awesome in glorious deeds, doing wonders?" And a definitive conclusion is given later in Jeremiah: "There is none like you, O LORD; you are great, and your name is great in might" (10:6).

How were the Israelites able to speak with such great certainty about God's holiness? All through their journey to the Promised Land and in the centuries that followed, they had witnessed His holiness up close. They had seen, with their own eyes, God's judgments against those who chose to be unholy.

One of the most sobering statements in all of Scripture is this: "Strive for peace with everyone, and for the holiness without which no one will see the Lord" (Hebrews 12:14). If God is, in His very essence, separate from us and rightly removed from anything and anyone lesser, how do we, as sinful and *un*holy beings, journey with Him?

Don't skip this; it matters. So often we make the mistake of thinking of God's holiness religiously rather than relationally. We can be transactional about His holiness and miss the wonder of how His holiness impacts our everyday lives.

Without God's holiness, how could we trust in His faithfulness? Without God's holiness, we would question His goodness. Without God's holiness, He could not be both kind and just. He would not be ruler *and* friend. He would not allow us to despair in our sin *and* hope in redemption. Without God's holiness, what is said about Him would not be true. These characteristics are what they are only because God is holy.

But even more amazing than that, unlike any other in all of God's creation, we are created *in His image*. As image-bearers, we are the *imago dei*. Human beings are the only ones created capable of reflecting the holiness of God. Does that blow your mind? That's how special and unique we are in relationship to God.

There is none
like you, O Lord;
you are great,
and your name
is great in
might.

JEREMIAH 10:6

THE HOLINESS OF GOD

In His holiness, God is separate from all things. He is transcendent above all, and He is absolutely, morally perfect, totally separated from sin. In every way, He is pure and set apart, and His desire is that we would set ourselves apart for Him. The devastating effects of sin on our world should lead us to realize the seriousness of sin and remind us of the urgency of holy living.

Sin marred our original intended capacity to image Him, and redemption through the grace of God restored it. In Christ, our capacity is shaped, refined, and perfected day by day through the process of sanctification. The grace of God transforms us into His likeness so that we not only experience His holiness but are able to reflect it ourselves.

John Piper, eager to pass on a greater awe and worship of God to the next generation, once defined God's holiness this way: "God's holiness is his infinite value as the absolutely unique, morally perfect, permanent person that he is and who by grace made himself accessible—his infinite value as the absolutely unique, morally perfect, permanent person that he is."[15]

God is like no one else. He is otherworldly and infinitely everything we were made to worship and long for. If it's true that God is this unique, this wonderful, and this available to us, then His holiness is not something that removes us far from Him, but is the reason we can be brought near. "By grace" is the intersection at which God's holiness mingles with God's mercy—His love with His justice. Without the grace of God, we would have no place in His holy presence—a truth illuminated in this familiar refrain:

Holy, holy, holy! though the darkness hide Thee,
Though the eye of sinful man Thy glory may not see;
Only Thou art holy; there is none beside Thee,
Perfect in power, love and purity.

Piper went on to conclude that passion for God's holiness or "infinite value" would sever and destroy our love for the world. And by personal experience, I know he's right. In my journey with God, the greater and brighter view I've had of His holiness, the dimmer worldly charms have become. My desire for my own holiness is directly proportional to valuing His. If God's holiness is what we were created to know through relationship with Him, then His holiness never leaves us unchanged.

The Lord Himself said to Moses in Leviticus 19:2, "You shall be holy, for I the LORD your God am holy." *But how?*

I simply can't imagine the weight of these words falling upon Moses. How is this even possible? How does one become holy like Him—He whose glory and holiness cannot be seen except for in passing while God hides you in the cleft of a rock?

The answer is the same. This side of the cross, we see that God's holiness never changed, but that He sent His Son, Christ, to be our covering. This side of the cross, we who are in Christ don't hide in fear of His holiness; we are *made holy* because Christ is holy.

Do you feel discouraged by your lack of growth and progress in this season? Are you tempted to shrink back in guilt or not-enoughness when faced with the truth of God's holiness? Don't look away and don't turn back; the more you grasp God's holiness, the more God's holiness will take hold of you. Take heart: If you're a pilgrim, journeying with Christ, you are

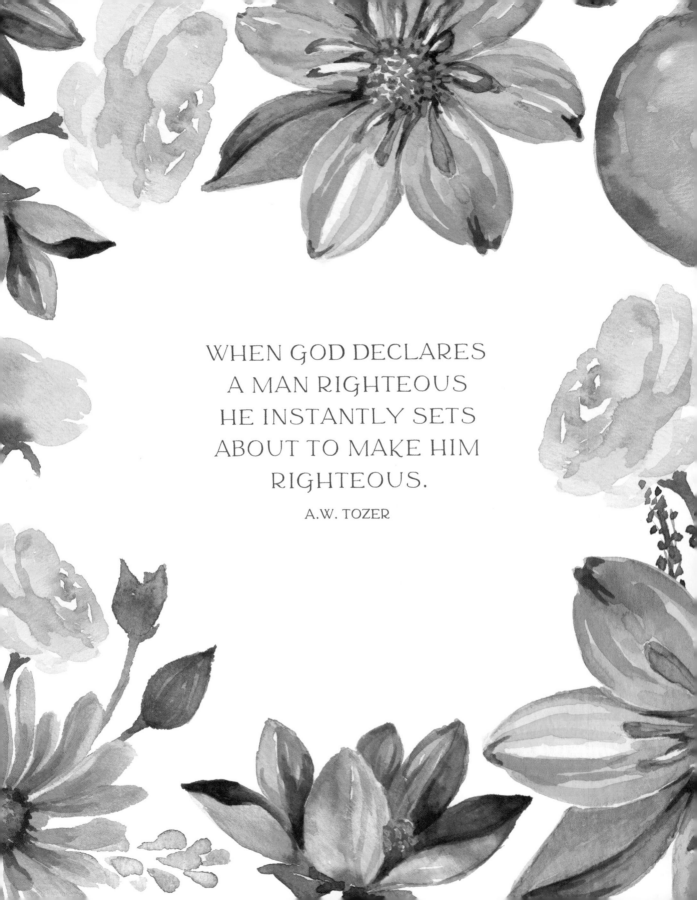

WHEN GOD DECLARES
A MAN RIGHTEOUS
HE INSTANTLY SETS
ABOUT TO MAKE HIM
RIGHTEOUS.

A.W. TOZER

set apart—made otherworldy—and transformed day by day into His likeness. This is who you are because holiness is who He is. You are a child of a holy God, and as we behold God's holiness, our passions for the distractions of this world fade away.

GUIDEPOST:

AS WE BEHOLD GOD'S HOLINESS, OUR PASSIONS FOR THE DISTRACTIONS OF THIS WORLD FADE AWAY.

Ever singing, march we onward, Victors in the midst of strife, Joyful music leads us sunward in the triumph song of life.

21

JOY FOR THE JOURNEY

Not far from us is an off-roading trail called Black Bear, which we drive as a family. (Just to be clear: I'm no outdoor adventurer; I'm just a six-time boy mom.) The trail begins off the highway on Red Mountain Pass in the San Juan Mountains, and ends in Telluride, Colorado. This jeep trail is not for beginners; in fact, it warns travelers of its technical difficulty with signs along the way, including a final sign that indicates, "One way only from this point on." I can't quite remember, but it may even say something like, "If you're scared now, there's no turning back later" (or maybe that's just what I think it ought to say after surviving the trail a few times now). Like most jeep trails, it climbs and winds through steep terrain, and then begins its descent along rugged narrow patches of road alongside cliffs and down jagged rocks and boulders. A suitable four-wheel-drive vehicle, great brakes, and careful focus on every twist and turn is a must. This is not a journey for mistakes or missteps.

Somewhere along the way, I usually get anxious and start questioning the wisdom or validity of such an adventure. How is this worth the stress? Why did we have to go over the mountain? Couldn't we have gone around instead? Where's the joy in the journey when the journey is this hard?

Just about the time these questions and frustrations surface, I get out of the car and start walking the trail by foot while Troy continues to drive carefully down the mountain. As I take my eyes off

203

GOD AS CREATOR

God created everything that exists, and when He surveyed the completed work of creation, He said, "It was very good." Psalm 139:13-16 says that God Himself formed you—that you are fearfully and wonderfully made. With the same care that He crafted you, He will sustain you—and He will conform you to the image of Christ. God's glory is the supreme purpose of all that He is doing and will do through you! (Ephesians 1:12).

the road and stop focusing on how accurately we're navigating the journey, I look up and grasp with clarity why we're traversing this rugged path: These are some of the most majestic vistas and displays of God's handiwork in all the world. The grandeur takes my breath away. My anxious thoughts are suddenly drowned out by the chorus of praise that involuntarily rises up in me when I'm confronted by God the Creator and the work of His hands.

In that moment, I know beyond a shadow of doubt that we were created for praise:

All Thy works with joy surround Thee,
Earth and heav'n reflect Thy rays,
Stars and angels sing around Thee,
Center of unbroken praise.
Field and forest, vale and mountain,
Flow'ry meadow, flashing sea,
Chanting bird and flowing fountain
Call us to rejoice in Thee!

Mortals, join the mighty chorus,
Which the morning stars began;
Father love is reigning o'er us,
Draws us through the Son of Man.
Ever singing, march we onward,
Victors in the midst of strife,
Joyful music leads us sunward
In the triumph song of life.

PRAISE IS THE REHEARSAL
OF OUR ETERNAL SONG.
BY GRACE WE LEARN TO SING,
AND IN GLORY
WE CONTINUE TO SING.

C.H. SPURGEON

These lyrics are more like a wake-up call than a pious declaration for a pilgrim lacking joy in his or her journey. It's as if these words were penned to urge the weary traveler in the midst of strife: Don't even think about quitting; the God who created all the earth is worthy of praise. And praise will shape your journey home.

> Oh come, let us sing to the LORD;
>> let us make a joyful noise to the rock of our salvation!
> Let us come into his presence with thanksgiving;
>> let us make a joyful noise to him with songs of praise!
>> (Psalm 95:1-2).

It's only natural to overflow with praise when the skies are blue and the road ahead is clear of all obstructions. Who can lack joy when good gifts, rich fare, and friends aplenty are before you? Who can withhold praise in times of ease and comfort? But in the midst of difficulties, trials, heartaches, and the unknown, how do we come and stay in God's presence with thanksgiving and joyful praise?

Perhaps God's awe-inspiring creation has something to do with His pursuit of our praise. He didn't have to create a sky that melts into sherbet-like pinks and oranges at day's end, but He did. He didn't have to fashion a bird with melodic voice, but even the faintest tune sung by the smallest of creation can call a day into order and our hearts to wonder. The budding leaves in spring, the icicles that form in winter, the carpet of golden leaves each autumn brings. The majestic mountain peaks, the endless fields of poppies, the galaxies of stars that sparkle at night—all of creation proclaims the Maker's praise...if we listen, if we adjust our view, if we pay attention. Our Creator, God, didn't have to design with intricate detail, or woo our senses through His handiwork, but He did.

If the praise on our lips follows the affections of our hearts, then we will grow to praise what we teach our hearts to love. I think that's why our good God didn't just form the earth but designed creation to capture our hearts and draw out our praise. God literally places guideposts of His grace throughout nature that display His care and handiwork in the world He created. It's humbling when you think about it. No wonder the apostle Paul wrote in Acts 17:24-25,

> The God who made the world and everything in it, being Lord of heaven and earth, does not live in temples made by man, nor is he served by human hands, as though

he needed anything, since he himself gives to all mankind life and breath and everything.

Humility and praise go hand in hand. It's in the very humbling, more-than-we-can-handle circumstances of our lives that we fall to our knees and look up. Do you feel gripped with fear on the road you're on? Have you been so focused on getting around the obstacles in your life that you've missed the joy in the journey? Take your eyes off of the seemingly impossible path ahead and take a moment to observe how God is at work all around you.

When we pay attention to the way God alone holds all things together in creation and in the created, even the most difficult parts of our journeys become opportunities to lift our eyes and our hearts in praise. It's what God purposed for us, His created.

Spurgeon said it well: "Praise is the rehearsal of our eternal song. By grace we learn to sing, and in glory we continue to sing."[16]

When we bow our hearts to our great Creator God, our hearts are, in turn, tuned to sing praises to Him. Praise realigns us with God's melody rather than our own—the melody intended for us in harmony with God, forevermore. Praise isn't simply a means to ease our journey; it is both our fuel and the destination. God's glorious creation stands as a constant reminder that He is at work all around us.

GUIDEPOST:

GOD'S GLORIOUS CREATION STANDS AS A CONSTANT REMINDER THAT HE IS AT WORK ALL AROUND US.

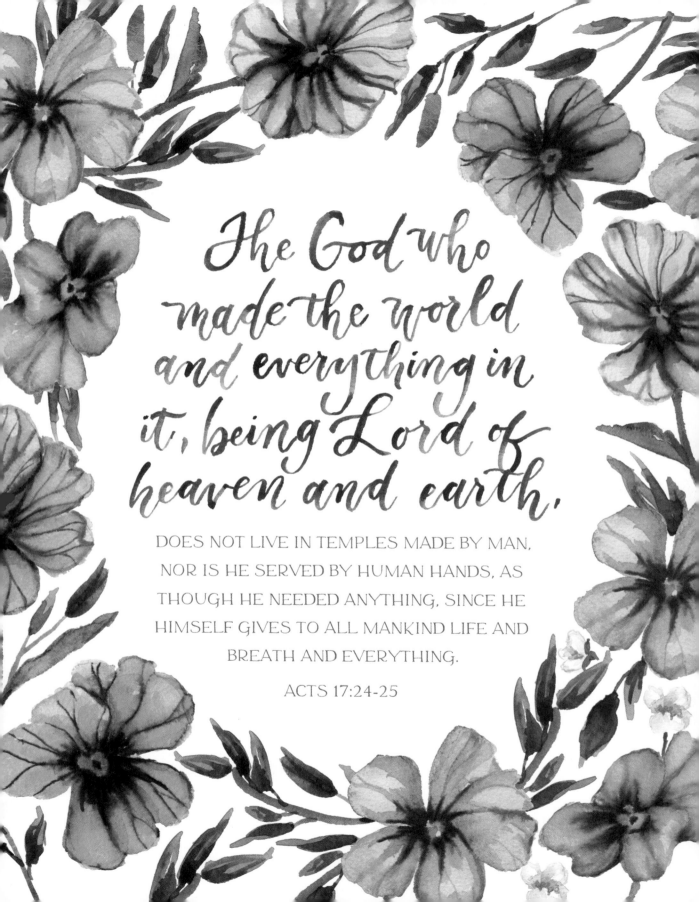

The God who made the world and everything in it, being Lord of heaven and earth,

DOES NOT LIVE IN TEMPLES MADE BY MAN, NOR IS HE SERVED BY HUMAN HANDS, AS THOUGH HE NEEDED ANYTHING, SINCE HE HIMSELF GIVES TO ALL MANKIND LIFE AND BREATH AND EVERYTHING.

ACTS 17:24-25

IN CHRIST ALONE
MY HOPE IS FOUND,

HE IS MY LIGHT,
MY STRENGTH, MY SONG;

THIS CORNERSTONE,
THIS SOLID GROUND,

FIRM THROUGH THE FIERCEST
DROUGHT AND STORM.

WHAT HEIGHTS OF LOVE,
WHAT DEPTHS OF PEACE,

WHEN FEARS ARE STILLED,
WHEN STRIVINGS CEASE,

MY COMFORTER,
MY ALL IN ALL,

HERE IN THE LOVE OF
CHRIST I STAND.

22

SOLID GROUND FOR LIFE'S STORMS

When you journey by boat to waters you're not familiar with, anchoring the boat so it stays safe and secure in one spot can be a challenge. If you can't tell how deep the water is or whether the bottom is covered in sand or rocks, you are left hoping that you have enough rope and that you're equipped with the right kind of anchor for getting a good grip on the bottom. Without a good hold, the anchor will drag, never secured to the solid ground of the earth beneath the water. Without anchoring properly or securely, your vessel will be at the mercy of the elements, and will travel and drift with the wind and the waves...in a direction you never intended to go.

Sometimes we don't realize how far adrift we've gone until we finally look up and realize we're nowhere near our target. Sometimes the traversing off course happens in small, seemingly insignificant ways. But tiny degrees of change add up to major trajectories of change. How many times do we find ourselves more consumed by the news than we intended, just to find our hearts eventually hardened and anxious by the course our thoughts have taken as a result? Or perhaps social media and endless scrolling have been the source of some drifting unanchored in a sea of popular opinion and approval. Or perhaps for some of us, the tether of God's Word has been loosely tied and only sporadically, and we're beginning to notice the effects of not being firmly anchored in our current season.

The writer of Hebrews wrote clearly about our need and access to a sure anchor:

> We have this as a sure and steadfast anchor of the soul, a hope that enters into the inner place behind the curtain (Hebrews 6:19).

As the writer of Hebrews goes on to explain, the hope that enters behind the curtain is Jesus Christ. He is our anchor, and here's why: For so long, only the high priest could enter the Holy of Holies in the temple to make the appropriate sacrifices to atone for and seek forgiveness of the sins of the Israelites. And he had to do this repeatedly.

But when Jesus bore on the cross the sins of all who would believe, He secured our access to God the Father once and for all. The curtain through which the high priest entered God's presence was divinely torn, signifying the removal of separation from a holy God and the granting of forgiveness for all that we could not atone for in our own power. Jesus is the hope that anchors us in the sea of doubt, fear, and impossible standards of right living apart from Christ.

We need to anchor ourselves to Christ, the solid rock. He is the immovable, unshakeable ground beneath the tumultuous sea we navigate. Anchoring to Him enables us to build our lives upon the rock that holds firm regardless of circumstances.

Stuart Townend's modern hymn "In Christ Alone" declares some of the most comforting and truth-filled lyrics in our generation:

> *In Christ alone my hope is found,*
> *He is my light, my strength, my song;*
> *This Cornerstone, this solid Ground,*
> *Firm through the fiercest drought and storm.*
> *What heights of love, what depths of peace,*
> *When fears are stilled, when strivings cease!*
> *My Comforter, my All in All,*
> *Here in the love of Christ I stand.*

The word *cornerstone* is a building and construction term. It refers to the foundation stone or base upon which two walls are joined and an entire structure is built upon. In the Sermon on the Mount, Jesus taught about two builders and their houses. A storm came and hit both structures at the same time. Above ground, the two houses may have appeared identical. They both

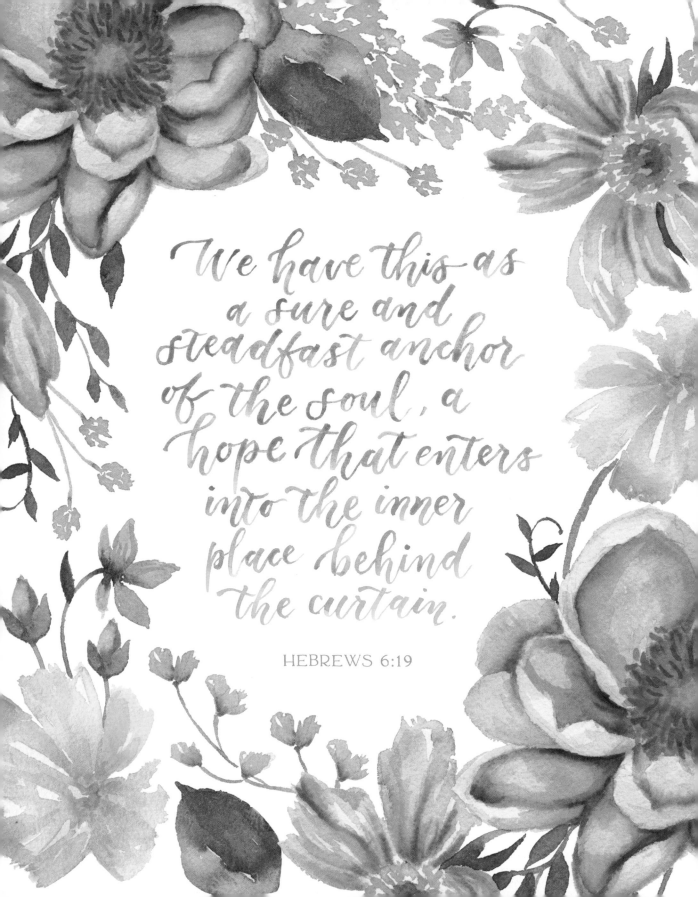

We have this as a sure and steadfast anchor of the soul, a hope that enters into the inner place behind the curtain.

HEBREWS 6:19

Cornerstone

CHRIST THE CORNERSTONE

When we build our lives upon Christ, the solid rock, we ensure that we will be safe and secure no matter what happens in life. When we anchor ourselves to Him, we won't be tossed to and fro by our circumstances. Rather, He will enable us to persevere and reach our heavenly destination.

looked sturdy and well made. But, according to Jesus' parable, the difference was the foundation upon which the houses stood. One builder built on rock (he acted on God's Word), while the other built on sand (he did not act on God's Word). Building upon the rock equals obeying God's Word and setting one's hope upon it. But building on sand is like being a hearer of the Word only and not a doer, according to James 1:22-24.

The illustrations of both the anchor and the house built on the rock are meant to help us grasp the seriousness—and serious blessing—of being grounded in Christ. To anchor or to build—both require us to take action. Neither is passive. We're not firmly anchored without intention. We do not build a house that stands without choosing a solid foundation.

Christ may be the solid rock we truly need, but if we haven't built ourselves on Him—if we are hearers only and not doers, loosely affiliated but not tethered—we will collapse and capsize under life's storms.

Today is a good day to assess your journey, pilgrim. Are you where you need to be? Have you built on the solid rock of Christ? Are you firmly anchored? If your answer is no to either or both, you are not alone, and it's not too late for you to correct course. Your Savior—who made a way for you to cease striving in your own strength, to stop being your own ship's captain, and to no longer need to try to build your life on your religious efforts—offers Himself as your steadfast anchor and the solid ground upon which you can stand. When we receive this gift of hope, nothing—no storm or turmoil—can separate us from our unshakeable rest in Him:

> *No guilt in life, no fear in death,*
> *This is the power of Christ in me;*
> *From life's first cry to final breath,*

Jesus commands my destiny.
No power of hell, no scheme of man,
Can ever pluck me from His hand:
Till He returns or calls me home,
Here in the power of Christ I'll stand.

Friend, don't be mistaken: The unshakable, solid ground of Christ is not merely a temporary help in a tumultuous season; it's meant to be the cornerstone of your whole life. When we build our lives upon Him, we rest assured and stand secure. When Christ is our cornerstone, even life's worst storms cannot collapse us.

GUIDEPOST:

WHEN CHRIST IS OUR CORNERSTONE, EVEN LIFE'S WORST STORMS CANNOT COLLAPSE US.

NEARING HOME

Let the Kingdom be always before you,
and believe with certainty and consistency
the things that are yet unseen.
Let nothing that is on this side of eternal life get inside you.

John Bunyan, *The Pilgrim's Progress*

Awake, my soul,
and sing of Him
who died for thee,
And hail Him as
thy matchless
King through
all eternity.

23

WORTHY BEYOND COMPARE

My husband, Troy, often reminds our family that life is practice for what we'll get to do for all eternity: Worship. He likes to say, "How do we expect to worship God for all eternity if it's foreign to us right now?" He usually brings this up with me when I feel particularly discouraged in the mundane everyday of life, or conversely, when I'm chasing big things and allowing myself to be a little too preoccupied with my own version of what my time on earth ought to look like.

Troy's simple summary is meant to convict *and* encourage, and once I get past the sting of how easy it is to worship myself instead of the holy God of the universe, I am deeply encouraged. I know he's right. Somehow, this one simple statement helps me reset and remember (with joy) that I was created to praise the King of kings, not to garner praise for myself with this one precious life. It reminds me that life's journey isn't *for us*, while heaven is for God; no, *it's ALL for Him*.

This is what we read about our Lord in the book of Revelation:

> On his robe and on his thigh he has a name written, King of kings and Lord of lords (19:16).

221

Jesus truly is the matchless King. As the Almighty, He is incomparable in every way—in His power, His wisdom, His love, His justice, His goodness. There is no greater sovereign we could ask to rule over us. Everything that a king should be, Jesus is. No wonder we will cast our heavenly crowns at His feet!

God is the matchless King, and He is continually on the throne, whether we acknowledge it, feel like it, or not. The doubling we see in the phrase "King of kings" was a practice of the Persians and Parthians to emphasize the supremacy of their royalties. The Messiah alone has a rightful claim to the title "King of kings and Lord of lords."

That Jesus is King of kings and Lord of lords means that He will rule supreme forever:

> I saw in the night visions, and behold, with the clouds of heaven there came one like a son of man, and he came to the Ancient of Days and was presented before him. And to him was given dominion and glory and a kingdom, that all peoples, nations, and languages should serve him; his dominion is an everlasting dominion, which shall not pass away, and his kingdom one that shall not be destroyed (Daniel 7:13-14).

And that all will bow to Him:

> At the name of Jesus every knee should bow, in heaven and on earth and under the earth, and every tongue confess that Jesus Christ is Lord, to the glory of God the Father (Philippians 2:10-11).

When during life's journey the world chases unending paths to self-discovery, identity, and self-love, it's ultimately hoping to find something worthy of worship—something worthy of the deep longing we have to be satisfied and fulfilled. As Christ-followers, we follow Christ, instead, because He is worthy. How do we know? Because the Bible declares it from beginning to end. The problem is that we often forget to practice now what we are meant to experience for all eternity: presence of God and worship of Him alone. We're quick to serve Him, but slow to

...SO THAT AT THE NAME OF JESUS EVERY KNEE SHOULD BOW, IN HEAVEN AND ON EARTH AND UNDER THE EARTH, AND EVERY TONGUE CONFESS THAT JESUS CHRIST IS LORD, TO THE GLORY OF GOD THE FATHER.

PHILIPPIANS 2:10-11

surrender in worship...prodigal with our ministry activities, events, and volunteerism, but miserly with the true consecration of our lives.

We would do well to daily rehearse how unique, awe-inspiring, and worthy of worship God is. Consider these words about the seraphim in Isaiah 6:

> Each one had six wings: two to cover his face, two to cover his feet, and two to fly, to carry out the will of the One worshiped. I wonder why he did not fly with six? If you gave most Christians today six wings, what would they want to do? Go as fast as they could! But where?

> Oh, no, four are to prepare for worship; only two are for service... It is always the same order: worship before service.[17]

The point: God desires worship before service.

It's in worship that we posture our hearts in humility and rightly align our will with His. It's through worship that we experience what we, the created, were meant to know in fullness and satisfaction. It's in worshipping our matchless King that we discover that nothing else compares.

Jesus was clear in His teaching: We can't serve two masters. There can be only one King and Ruler of our lives—and most often, that means dethroning ourselves. But what if submitting and surrendering to the King of kings puts everything else properly in its place? Do you struggle with self-esteem—with feeling unworthy? Friend, what you and I need is not greater self-worth; we need to be overwhelmed by the worthiness of Christ.

What if the very worthiness we've been chasing on our pilgrim journey is achieved first and foremost because God calls us His own? The wonder of redemption is that God created us for Himself; so when we praise Him, rest in Him, and find our identities in who He says we are, all other

empty pursuits lose their appeal in comparison to the satisfaction of worshipping our King:

> *Crown Him with many crowns,*
> *The Lamb upon His throne;*
> *Hark! how the heav'nly anthem drowns*
> *All music but its own:*
> *Awake, my soul, and sing*
> *Of Him who died for thee,*
> *And hail Him as thy matchless King*
> *Through all eternity.*

What a difference it makes when I preach these well-penned hymn lyrics to myself: *Awake, my soul, and sing of Him who gave everything to rescue you. Don't even try and chase after anything else; He alone is worthy and His faithfulness unmatched.*

This is the kind of rehearsal Troy is talking about when he reminds me to practice what I'll be doing for all eternity.

As Paul David Tripp says, "The Bible isn't a storybook with many heroes. No, there's only one hero in Scripture: the Son, the Lamb, the Savior, the King, the Redeemer—Jesus."[18] There is no one like Him. This matchless King, Jesus, *is* the hero of our pilgrim story, and we will dwell in His presence, and sing praises to Him for all eternity. Get ready...and start right now. Because Jesus is the King of kings, He rules over every circumstance we face.

GUIDEPOST:

BECAUSE JESUS IS THE KING OF KINGS, HE RULES OVER EVERY CIRCUMSTANCE WE FACE.

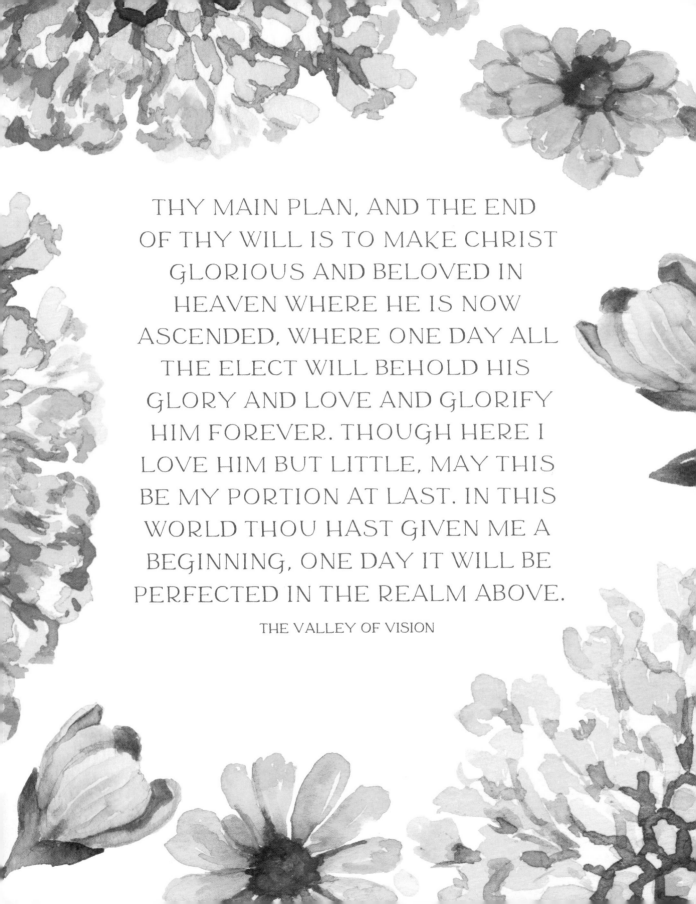

THY MAIN PLAN, AND THE END OF THY WILL IS TO MAKE CHRIST GLORIOUS AND BELOVED IN HEAVEN WHERE HE IS NOW ASCENDED, WHERE ONE DAY ALL THE ELECT WILL BEHOLD HIS GLORY AND LOVE AND GLORIFY HIM FOREVER. THOUGH HERE I LOVE HIM BUT LITTLE, MAY THIS BE MY PORTION AT LAST. IN THIS WORLD THOU HAST GIVEN ME A BEGINNING, ONE DAY IT WILL BE PERFECTED IN THE REALM ABOVE.

THE VALLEY OF VISION

So I'll cherish the old rugged cross

TILL MY TROPHIES AT LAST I LAY DOWN;
I WILL CLING TO THE OLD RUGGED CROSS,
AND EXCHANGE IT SOMEDAY FOR A CROWN.

24

MORE THAN ENOUGH

The cross of Christ is an intersection, both figuratively and quite literally. An instrument of death in the ancient world—formed by two perpendicular wooden beams that intersect—it poignantly represents the crossroads of decision we're faced with when we consider the finished work of redemption on the cross, where Jesus bore our sin. At this intersection, one chooses whether to continue down the path he or she is already on, or to turn and go a different direction.

The cross of Christ is the hinge on which all of human history turns—it is the point at which mankind no longer needed to despair in hopelessness from the burden of sin and death. It was the literal way God chose to sacrifice His Son and redeem His sons and daughters to Himself. When it comes to the cross, where Jesus completed the work of forgiveness and love that His Father had sent Him to do, every person is at a crossroads of decision: the choice to either reject His invitation or surrender to His provision. You can't truly encounter the person of Jesus and not evaluate which direction you're heading.

For those who are believers, the emblem is familiar: it's the old rugged cross.

But maybe the story of redemption feels far in the distant past for us, from a time when life seemed simpler and faith felt fresh. Perhaps the daily noise keeps us buzzing along, but the still and quiet moments of a day's end bring to the surface the decisions we're otherwise too distracted to engage.

For us, the cross was a moment of decision with a lifetime of benefits. But even now—on our journeys with Christ—we can be tempted to wonder if the current crossroads we're facing in life require something...*more*.

What really matters? What needs to change in my life? What am I living for? How do I make my life count?

Truth be told, we so often turn to friends, social media, or our digital devices for the answers we seek. We can come to think of the cross of Christ as that good news in our moment of crisis long ago and forget that Jesus is meant to be the good news for all our days, and for every path or crossroads we face thereafter.

The answers we seek at the crossroads we encounter all through the journey will find resolution and rest only when we look to Jesus, hope in the cross, and journey *with Christ*:

Let us run with endurance the race that is set before us, looking to Jesus, the founder and perfecter of our faith, who for the joy that was set before him endured the cross, despising the shame, and is seated at the right hand of the throne of God (Hebrews 12:1-3).

The cross may be an old, familiar story in our lives, but it is more relevant to our immediate concerns and crossroads than we might think in this day of quick fixes and temporary salves. The writer of Hebrews sets the hope of Christ as our forerunner—the one who leads the way, charts the course, and provides for our perseverance. The cross of Christ is ever potent and is what makes it possible for us to run the race God has set before us.

Friend, *every* decision or life direction you and I face on this journey is shaped by how the cross shapes us. You may be weary, conflicted, confused, or unsure of your next steps, but in the shadow of the cross of our redemption, your path is sure and your true treasure is waiting.

LET US RUN WITH
ENDURANCE THE RACE
THAT IS SET BEFORE US,

looking to Jesus,
the founder and
perfecter of
our faith

HEBREWS 12:1-2

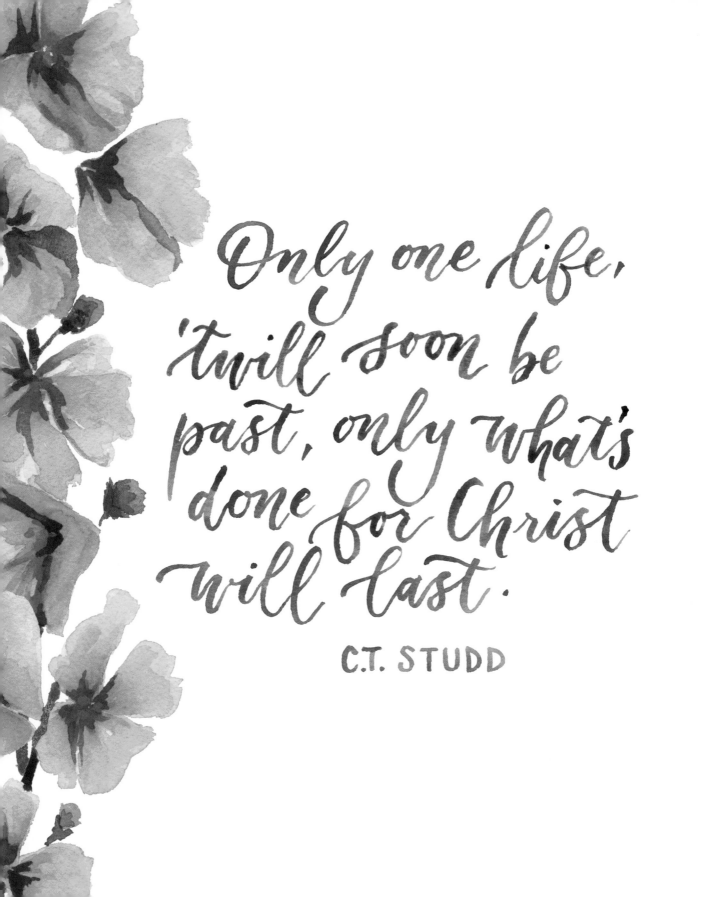

Only one life,
'twill soon be
past, only what's
done for Christ
will last.

C.T. STUDD

THE FINISHED WORK OF CHRIST

The cross is the turning point of all human history. It was there that Christ offered up a once-for-all sacrifice that made our redemption possible. He accomplished what we could not; without the cross, we would not be pilgrims destined for heaven. Christ did it all, and He should be our all.

As the beloved hymn professes:

So I'll cherish the old rugged cross,
Till my trophies at last I lay down;
I will cling to the old rugged cross,
And exchange it someday for a crown.

"Jesus is better," we say, but do we believe it and live as if He is all we have? Do we know Him to be so much worthier than any trophy or treasure we could gain on this earth? Are we clinging to our hope in Christ—running with endurance with our eyes set on Him—or are we clinging to the worldly comforts and accolades we've accumulated along the way? Randy Alcorn says it like this: "He who lays up treasures on earth spends his life backing away from his treasures. To him, death is loss. He who lays up treasures in heaven looks forward to eternity; he's moving daily toward his treasures. To him, death is gain."[19]

What might the path before us look like if we took each step of our race believing there is no greater destination than that of knowing and growing in Christ?

The truth is, all will pass away on this journey of life except for what is done in the name of Christ. Even the apostle Paul declared,

> Indeed, I count everything as loss because of the surpassing worth of knowing Christ Jesus my Lord. For his sake I have suffered the loss of all things and count them as rubbish, in order that I may gain Christ and be found in him, not having a righteousness of my own that comes from the law, but that which comes through faith in Christ, the righteousness from God that

depends on faith—that I may know him and the power of his resurrection, and may share his sufferings, becoming like him in his death (Philippians 3:8-10).

My pilgrim friend, every guidepost thus far has aimed to point weary Christ-following believers like me and you to the unchanging truths of God's character and the evidence of His grace along the windy roads of our journeys with Him. These biblical truths are meant to remind us that we don't travel alone, and to encourage us to persevere all the way to our destination. This pilgrim journey is a continual tethering of head and heart, mind and body, trust and obedience. We've come so far together. And I want you to know this: If there is one truth that will serve us every step of the way, it's that Christ's finished work on the cross is what makes it possible for us to complete the journey. That's it.

Christ is all, and all we could ever truly hope for. Every attribute of God and evidence of His grace is found in the God-man, Jesus Christ. Every guidepost that points us to God's faithful presence points us to Jesus.

So, do you see that old rugged cross? It always was and always will be more than enough.

GUIDEPOST:

CHRIST'S FINISHED WORK ON THE CROSS IS WHAT MAKES IT POSSIBLE FOR US TO COMPLETE THE JOURNEY.

WHEN ON THE DAY THE GREAT I AM, THE
FAITHFUL AND THE TRUE

THE LAMB WHO WAS FOR SINNERS SLAIN, IS
MAKING ALL THINGS NEW.

BEHOLD OUR GOD SHALL LIVE WITH US
AND BE OUR STEADFAST LIGHT,

AND WE SHALL E'ER HIS PEOPLE BE, ALL
GLORY BE TO CHRIST!

25

ARRIVING HOME

od is going to do big things with your life," we often hear. No doubt well meaning, but is it true? Is it *big* when God allows a believer to wrestle with debilitating chronic illness? Is it *big* when a godly servant spends his or her life serving in a small one-room church in a rural town? Is it *big* when a mother turns down a corner-office promotion to teach her children full time from home? Can a small and hidden life be as glorious as one seen and heard across the globe?

While not big by earthly standards, even small acts of obedience that go unnoticed can be big displays of God's glory. You see, God *is* doing big things when redeemed lives, no longer living for themselves, bring Him glory.

If I'm honest: There are days when you can find me scheming big plans for my ideal life and thinking more of myself than I ought. This posture is the source of 99.99 percent of my discontent and worry, and my guess is that you often see the same in your life too. I'm always miserable when I forget who's in charge of the journey I'm on.

What makes something big or noteworthy? Dollars? Followers? Influence? Fame? In the hustle and hurry of our daily walk with God, it's easy to convince ourselves that we're simply trying to make the most of our lives when we're actually wooed by earthly glory rather than His. It's hard to be consumed with God's glory when we're busy trying to acquire our own.

THE GLORY OF GOD

We could never sufficiently define God's glory because the extent of His glory is beyond our comprehension, but we can begin to grasp what it involves by realizing that He is infinitely great, beautiful, perfect, and holy. These attributes and more make Him eminently worthy of our praise and worship. And it's as we do everything with a deliberate intent to honor and exalt Him that we become active participants in bringing Him glory.

It's difficult to define God's glory, but this is helpful:

The glory of God is the manifest beauty of his holiness. It is the going-public of his holiness. It is the way he puts his holiness on display for people to apprehend. So, the glory of God is the holiness of God made manifest.[20]

Simply put, the summation of everything that makes God the definition of truth, beauty, holiness, and goodness radiates as God's divine glory, and ultimately, we get to experience and participate in it.

It's eternal light overcoming darkness:

The city has no need of sun or moon to shine on it, for the glory of God gives it light, and its lamp is the Lamb. By its light will the nations walk, and the kings of the earth will bring their glory into it, and its gates will never be shut by day—and there will be no night there. They will bring into it the glory and the honor of the nations. But nothing unclean will ever enter it, nor anyone who does what is detestable or false, but only those who are written in the Lamb's book of life (Revelation 21:23-27).

It's the picture of grace and truth:

The Word became flesh and dwelt among us, and we have seen his glory, glory as of the only Son from the Father, full of grace and truth (John 1:14).

It's seen in God's handiwork:

The heavens declare the glory of God,
    and the sky above proclaims his handiwork (Psalm 19:1).

For from him and through him and to him are all things. To him be glory forever.

ROMANS 11:36

It permeates everything:

> And one called to another and said:
>> "Holy, holy, holy is the LORD of hosts;
>> the whole earth is full of his glory!" (Isaiah 6:3).

The apostle Paul reminds believers in his letter to the Romans: "For from him and through him and to him are all things. To him be glory forever" (Romans 11:36).

This means that nothing we have, no circumstances we've been given, no talents we possess on this road with Christ have been entrusted to us for our own glory. They are all from Him, through Him, and *to* Him.

And then these familiar words rise to the surface of my thoughts:

> *Should nothing of our efforts stand, no legacy survive;*
> *Unless the Lord does raise the house, in vain its builders strive.*
> *To you who boast tomorrow's gain, tell me what is your life?*
> *A mist that vanishes at dawn, all glory be to Christ!*
> *All glory be to Christ our King.*
> *All glory be to Christ!*
> *His rule and reign we'll ever sing,*
>> *all glory be to Christ!*

I get tearful every time I begin to sing these opening lines to the hymn "All Glory Be to Christ." The truths reflected in these lines unmask the ache and weariness that so often accompanies us as we journey with Christ—simply because we forget that it's not about us.

Release and relief.

How do we get so caught up in believing this journey is all about us? The pressure's off, friend; all the glory belongs to Christ.

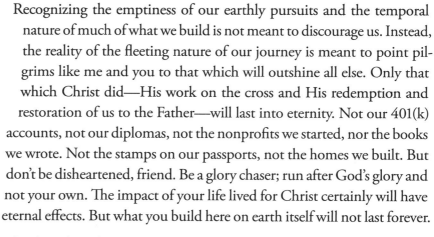

Recognizing the emptiness of our earthly pursuits and the temporal nature of much of what we build is not meant to discourage us. Instead, the reality of the fleeting nature of our journey is meant to point pilgrims like me and you to that which will outshine all else. Only that which Christ did—His work on the cross and His redemption and restoration of us to the Father—will last into eternity. Not our 401(k) accounts, not our diplomas, not the nonprofits we started, nor the books we wrote. Not the stamps on our passports, not the homes we built. But don't be disheartened, friend. Be a glory chaser; run after God's glory and not your own. The impact of your life lived for Christ certainly will have eternal effects. But what you build here on earth itself will not last forever.

What big plans does God have for our lives, then? That as those forgiven and sanctified in Christ, we—as Christ-followers—are His trophies, and our redeemed and praise-filled presence in heaven will bring Him glory—for eternity.

Any glory we could attain on this earth pales in comparison to the glory we get to bring Christ with our surrendered lives.

When on the day the great I Am, the Faithful and the True
The Lamb who was for sinners slain, is making all things new.
Behold our God shall live with us and be our steadfast light,
And we shall e'er His people be, all glory be to Christ!
All glory be to Christ, our King. All glory be to Christ!
His rule and reign we'll ever sing, all glory be to Christ!

His promise to make all things new (Revelation 21:5) includes remaking me and you. This is no small, insignificant purpose for our lives, friend. This is the Creator restoring us to the very likeness of Himself He intended for us and making us fit to bring Him glory—and fit to be glorified with Him. He has big plans for us, indeed.

Like the sunrise that comes over the horizon after a long night, may the glory of Christ be the warmth and light by which you and I run—or crawl, if we must—over the finish line of our pilgrim journey heavenward. He is the

Way, the Truth, and the Life, and our pilgrim journey knows no course but the story of redemption that God has written from before the beginning of time. We've never walked this road alone, and we never will. The declarations of God's grace are all around, and His forever grace will lead us all the way home.

GUIDEPOST:

GOD'S FOREVER GRACE WILL LEAD US ALL THE WAY HOME.

HYMNS CITED IN PILGRIM

NOTES

CITED IN THE TEXT

1. Carl R. Trueman, *Grace Alone—Salvation as a Gift of God* (Grand Rapids, MI: Zondervan, 2017), 24.

2. Corrie ten Boom with John and Elizabeth Sherrill, *The Hiding Place* (New York: Bantam, 1971), 217.

3. This statement is attributed to Thomas Watson, but the original source is unknown.

4. Timothy Keller, tweeted on April 25, 2013, https://twitter.com/timkellernyc/status/327444450064351233.

5. William Secker, *The Nonsuch Professor* (London: R.D. Dickinson, 1867), 139.

6. Attributed to C.H. Spurgeon, original source unknown.

7. A.W. Tozer, *Renewed Day by Day* (Camp Hill, PA: Wing Spread Publishers, 2010), June 5.

8. Jerry Bridges, *The Discipline of Grace* (Colorado Springs: NavPress, 2006), 88.

9. Joni Eareckson Tada, "Is God Really In Control?" (Joni and Friends, 1987), 1.

10. C.H. Spurgeon, *Morning by Morning* (London: Passmore and Alabaster, n.d.), November 2.

11. Paul David Tripp, *A Quest for More* (Greensboro, SC: New Growth Press, 2008), 107.

12. Matthew Henry, *An Exposition of All the Books of the Old and New Testaments, Vol. III* (London: W. Baynes, 1805), 364.

13. John Newton, "Amazing Grace," 1772.

14. Sam Storms, "The Dangers of Intimacy," https://www.samstorms.org/all-articles/post/dangers-of-intimacy.

15. John Piper, "How Do You Define God's Holiness?," *Desiring God*, November 3, 2017, https://www.desiringgod.org/messages/a-generation-passionate-for-gods-holiness/excerpts/how-do-you-define-gods-holiness.

16. C.H. Spurgeon, *Metropolitan Tabernacle Pulpit* (London: Passmore & Alabaster, 1890), 12.

17. Joseph S. Carroll, *How to Worship Jesus Christ* (Chicago, IL: Moody Publishers, 2013), 49.

18. Paul David Tripp, from a Facebook post in 2015, date unknown.

19. Randy Alcorn, "Where's Your Heart?," *Eternal Perspective Ministries*, May 11, 2016, https://www.epm.org/blog/2016/May/11/wheres-your-heart.

20. John Piper, "What Is God's Glory?," *Desiring God*, https://www.desiringgod.org/interviews/what-is-gods-glory—2.

QUOTES IN ART

Page 21—C.H. Spurgeon, *Six Sermons by the Rev. C.H. Spurgeon* (London: James Paul, 1856), 43.

Page 25—Matthew Henry, *An Exposition of the Old and New Testament, Vol. V* (New York: Robert Carter, 1856), 264.

Page 37—A.W. Tozer, *Knowledge of the Holy* (Zeeland, MI: Reformed Church Publications, 2015), 82.

Page 59—Thomas Adams, as cited in *The Westminster Collection of Christian Quotations*, comp. Martin H. Manser (Louisville, KY: Westminster John Knox Press, 2001), 169.

Page 63—Attributed to Thomas Watson, original source unknown.

Page 93—A.W. Tozer, *Evenings with Tozer* (Chicago, IL: Moody, 1981), August 4.

Page 109—Attributed to C.H. Spurgeon, original source unknown.

Page 121—Martin Luther, *Sermons of Martin Luther, Vol. 2* (Grand Rapids, MI: Baker, 1983), 72.

Page 133—Jen Wilkin, *In His Image* (Wheaton, IL: Crossway, 2018), 153.

Page 144—A.W. Tozer, *Jesus* (Chicago, IL: Moody, 2017), 104.

Page 155—Annie Johnson Flint, "He Giveth More Grace," year unknown, but Annie lived from 1866–1932.

Page 162—Widely attributed to Joni Eareckson Tada, but original source unknown.

Page 169—Sinclair Ferguson, "How Long Will It Last?," *Tabletalk* 28:5 (May 2004), 26-27.

Page 178—Matthew Henry, *An Exposition of All the Books of the Old and New Testaments, Vol. III* (London: W. Baynes, 1805), 364.

Page 187—William Carey, as cited in *The Missionary Review of the World* (New York: Funk & Wagnalls, 1900), 899.

Page 200—*Evenings with Tozer* (Chicago, IL: Moody, 2015), December 8.

Page 206—C.H. Spurgeon, *Metropolitan Tabernacle Pulpit* (London: Passmore & Alabaster, 1890), 12.

Page 229—Excerpted from *The Valley of Vision*, comp. Arthur Bennett (Carlisle, PA: Banner of Truth, 2003).

Page 234—Attributed to C.T. Studd, original source unknown.

Page 252—C.H. Spurgeon, *Evening by Evening* (London: Passmore & Alabaster, n.d.), April 9.

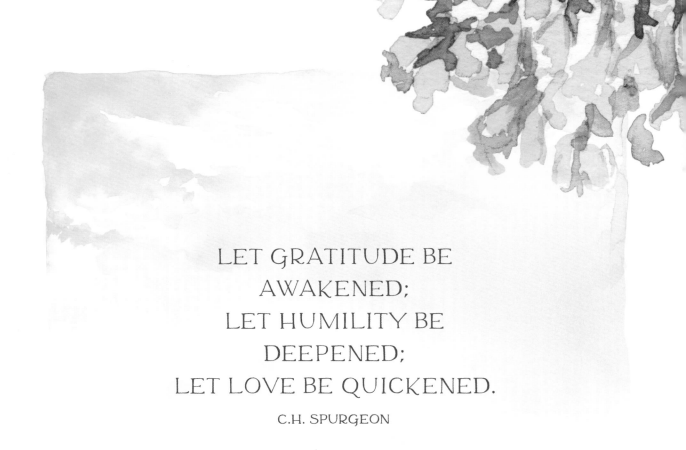

LET GRATITUDE BE
AWAKENED;
LET HUMILITY BE
DEEPENED;
LET LOVE BE QUICKENED.

C.H. SPURGEON

ACKNOWLEDGMENTS

I'm so grateful for the companions and co-laborers God brings alongside us in each of our journeys. Not only does the collaboration with others push the creative endeavor so much further, but the joy of delighting in God's faithfulness with co-laborers while stewarding gifts together is…well, unparalleled. I want to thank those who have made this particular journey both fruitful and deeply significant for me: My incredible team at Harvest House Publishers, especially Steve Miller, Sherrie Slopianka, and Janelle Coury, for helping me steward this vision and give it life; my agent, Jenni Burke, for championing my voice and point of view; my faithful team at GraceLaced; Eve Stipes, who cares for my words as if they were her own; Sarah Alexander Schools, who cares for my art as if it were her own; and to my Simons men—Troy and boys—I can't believe I get to journey with you. Finally, all thanks and praise be to Christ our King; His rule and reign we'll ever sing, all glory be to Christ.

ABOUT THE AUTHOR

Ruth Chou Simons is a bestselling and award-winning author of several books and Bible studies—including *GraceLaced*, *Beholding and Becoming*, and *When Strivings Cease*. She is an artist, entrepreneur, podcaster, and speaker, using each of these platforms to spiritually sow the Word of God into people's hearts. Through her online shoppe at GraceLaced.com and her social media community, Simons shares her journey of God's grace intersecting daily life with word and art. Ruth and her husband, Troy, are grateful parents to six sons—their greatest adventure.

OTHER BOOKS
BY RUTH